THE LAWYER'S GUIDE TO MENTORING

Ida O. Abbott, Esq.

Sponsored by the New York Women's Bar Association, Inc.

PUBLISHED BY THE
NATIONAL ASSOCIATION
FOR LAW PLACEMENT

Preface by Michael A. Cooper

PRESIDENT, ASSOCIATION OF THE
BAR OF THE CITY OF NEW YORK

DEDICATION

For Myles

Sponsored by the New York Women's Bar Association Foundation, Inc.
P.O. Box 31, Murray Hill Station
New York, NY 10156-0031
(212) 251-1344

Published by the National Association for Law Placement, Inc. (NALP)
1666 Connecticut Avenue NW, Suite 325
Washington, DC 20009-1039
(202) 667-1666 • Fax (202) 265-6735
Web site: www.nalp.org

ISBN: 1-55733-020-4

HISTORICAL NOTE

The word "mentor" derives from Greek mythology. In Homer's *The Odyssey*, the goddess Athena came to earth in the form of Mentor, a trusted friend of Odysseus. It was Mentor who cared for and advised Odysseus' son, Telemachus, during his father's long absence in the Trojan Wars. For generations, the term "mentor" has been based on this model of a wise and trusted teacher and advisor. Laurent A. Daloz, in his book, *Mentor: Guiding the Journey of Adult Mentors*, explains that this concept of the mentor is found not just in *The Odyssey*, but throughout the world's folklore and literature in such varied figures as fairy godmothers, Merlin, Dante's Virgil, the spider woman in Native American lore, Utnapishtim in the Gilgamesh epic, the Skin Horse in *The Velveteen Rabbit*, and Yoda in Star Wars. Daloz further explains that mentors take us on a journey: "We trust them because they have been there before. They embody our hopes, cast light on the way ahead, interpret arcane signs, warn us of lurking dangers, and point out unexpected delights along the way."

Although found in literary forms for centuries, the concept of mentors in the workplace is very recent. Research in this area began in the mid-1970s, about the time that women were entering the work force in record numbers, and the importance of mentors in business and industry was popularized in books like Gail Sheehy's *Passages*. Long associated with a type of person, the term "mentor" has only recently been used to refer to a process. In fact, the definition for "mentor" as a verb first appeared in *Webster's Dictionary* only in the early 1980s.

CONTENTS

FOREWORD

by The New York Women's Bar Association Foundation

The New York Women's Bar Association Foundation is proud to sponsor this essential "success guide" for mentors, protégés, and legal employers. Successful mentoring is a powerful tool for recruiting, growing, and retaining talented lawyers and achieving other important professional and business objectives.

For *protégés*, mentoring promotes on-the-job learning, work satisfaction, and career success. The higher productivity and reduced turnover of those being mentored translates into increased profitability for *legal employers*. For their part, *mentors* gain fresh perspectives from their protégés, find personal and professional renewal in the process of guiding others, and assure a more secure retirement by contributing to the future viability of their employer.

The Committee to Advance Women in the Profession of the New York Women's Bar Association (NYWBA) became interested in mentoring in the early 1990s for two reasons: first, because of the positive connection between mentoring and career success, and, second, because mentoring was then, and remains today, unavailable to most women and minority lawyers, especially in large firms. In the economic downturn of that period, the Committee observed that women lawyers were disproportionately affected by the massive law firm layoffs. We concluded that, just as the presence of mentoring promotes a lawyer's career, its absence is a substantial career deficit.

In 1994, the NYWBA launched a group mentoring program for its members based on examples of successful corporate, accounting firm, and not-for-profit mentoring programs. The program was based on a "multiple mentor" model in which protégés benefit from support

networks of advisors inside and outside their workplace instead of
having a single all-powerful office mentor who is expected to guide
their entire career. The program began with a kick-off and training
session at which mentoring objectives were identified,[1] group procedures were established, discussion topics were suggested, and the
groups met for the first time. At its peak there were 14 peer mentoring
groups involving a total of more than 100 participants. The procedures
established at the launch of the program continue today. No formal
pairings are made, and each group meets as a whole at least six times
during each one-year cycle. Within each group, participants are mixed
as to seniority, type of legal employment (firm, corporate, government,
non-profit), and practice area.

The participants' response has been overwhelmingly positive, as
measured by formal surveys, informal follow-up interviews, and the
fact that, after five years in operation, three of the original groups
continue to meet regularly and new groups have been added. In a
profession characterized by constant turnover, intense competitive pressures, and weakening loyalties to employers and colleagues, participants
showed unusual commitment to their mentoring groups. In a survey
conducted after the first cycle of the program, more than 75 percent of
participants said they valued the diversity of the groups and 60 percent
said that they functioned in their group both as mentor and mentee.

The administrative demands of the NYWBA program are light and
the operating costs are low. This *pro bono* effort was established by a
small committee of bar association members with demanding full-time
legal careers and is currently administered by a senior associate in the
litigation department of a large New York City law firm who also chairs
an active substantive committee of the Association of the Bar of the
City of New York.

The success of the NYWBA group mentoring program raises the
question of how the benefits of mentoring can be enjoyed by a
broader segment of the legal community. This book is part of the
answer. It demonstrates to lawyers and their employers nationwide —
whether law firms, corporate law departments, government agencies,
or others — (1) the benefits of mentoring at all career levels; (2) how

---

[1] They were: (1) assist in career and personal development, (2) provide insight for
career moves, (3) develop positive relationships with other female attorneys, and
(4) develop communication and networking skills.

individuals can mentor and be mentored effectively; and (3) how legal employers can implement successful mentoring programs by setting well-defined objectives, training mentors and protégés, providing incentives for participation, and continuously monitoring and evaluating outcomes.

Some employers target mentoring efforts to high-potential employees, women, or minority employees, but other employers who believe exclusionary groupings have too many negatives sponsor inclusive programs only. This is just one example of the choices that are available and the need for employers to identify their objectives and carefully tailor programs to meet those goals.

No one is better qualified than Ida Abbott to guide employers in this process and to bring to the legal profession the whys, wherefores, and how-tos of mentoring. Ida distilled the wisdom in this book from the "best practices" of existing models in business, education and other professions, and from her extensive experience as a consultant to legal employers on mentoring and other methods of professional and practice development. In this book Ida speaks to lawyers from an inside track based on her distinguished 20-year career as a lawyer and her work with law firms and legal organizations around the country. Before starting her consulting firm in 1995, Ida specialized in complex litigation and was in charge of lawyer training at Heller Ehrman White & McAuliffe in San Francisco. She currently chairs the Bar Association of San Francisco Law Practice Management Section and is on the Editorial Advisory Board of *Law Firm Governance*, for which she writes a column on professional development.

We hope *The Lawyer's Guide to Mentoring* will be read by all who wish to bring the very best practices, leadership, and vision to our rapidly changing profession.

January 2000

New York Women's Bar Association Foundation, Inc.

Gina S. Anderson, *Founder and Past President (1995-1999)*

Martha E. Gifford, *Founder and Vice President*

Jolie E. Schwab, *Member, Board of Directors*

PREFACE

by Michael A. Cooper, President
The Association of the Bar
of the City of New York

Serving as President of The Association of the Bar of the City of New York has afforded me numerous opportunities to talk with young lawyers, and it is dismaying to learn that many of them do not derive the same satisfaction, personal and professional, that I and most of my peers experienced when we were young lawyers. Some of our current counterparts are so disaffected that they are leaving not only their firms but the legal profession entirely, choosing instead to pursue other callings and lifestyles that they see as more attractive.

The financial incentives offered by law firms and other legal employers may provide sufficient motivation to remain during the initial years of one's career, but for many lawyers financial incentives are not alone sufficient over the long haul. A sense of fulfillment, rooted in doing challenging work in a collegial and supportive environment, is needed for lawyers to truly wish to remain with their employers. A strong, well-designed mentoring program can go a long way toward creating that environment.

Mentoring was a natural and widespread phenomenon three and four decades ago. I recall sitting with one of my firm's senior partners for three hours while he critiqued and improved a pleading I had drafted for his review; today our communication would probably be via e-mail. Other partners welcomed me into their homes and their families, giving an additional and much appreciated dimension to our working relationship. Those partners may not have thought that they were "mentoring" me, and I know I did not view them as fulfilling a specific "mentoring" function, though in retrospect I see that they clearly were.

There is less mentoring today because mentoring comes at a price — in time, attention and sympathetic interest — that too few senior lawyers seem willing to pay. Competitive pressures create a super-heated atmosphere in which the end product, be it a brief or merger agreement, not only overshadows but totally eclipses in significance the interactive process by which it was created and the professional and personal relationships among its creators.

Mentoring is important to the maturation and satisfaction of all young and not so young lawyers, but especially so for minority and women associates. All too frequently they feel alienated and uncon-nected to their contemporaries, and they are often among the first to leave a firm because they face barriers, real and perceived, without a helping hand to overcome them.

It must be clear by now that I believe there is a great and growing need for a book such as this. It provides a useful two-part guide to mentoring. The first part explains why mentoring matters and de-scribes the transformative role it can play, helping to turn inexperi-enced and insecure fledgling lawyers into accomplished and assured professionals. The second part describes the structural elements of a successful mentoring program, including alternatives and modifica-tions to tailor a program to a particular work setting.

We would all do well to learn the lessons of this book: that mentoring is valuable at various stages of a lawyer's professional development and can provide at a modest investment great rewards, not just for the mentored lawyer, but for the mentors and their organizations as a whole.

January 2000

Michael A. Cooper

Michael A. Cooper
President
The Association of the Bar of the City of New York

Acknowledgments

by the New York Women's Bar
Association Foundation

From our first reading of Ida Abbott's articles on mentoring in the legal profession, the New York Women's Bar Association Foundation knew we had found the perfect author for this book. In the course of publication we learned that our collaborator also has enormous energy, good humor, and generosity. There is no greater incentive than to work with others moved by the same spirit toward a common goal in the public good. This book is the product of such a relationship between Ida and the Foundation.

The Foundation had the good fortune to find in the National Association for Law Placement, and in Executive Director Paula A. Patton, a publisher whose educational mission is so closely allied to our own that we feel we are among family. Thanks to Janet Smith, NALP Director of Communications Media and Publications, for expertly shepherding the book through production.

The Foundation has been assisted greatly by The Association of the Bar of the City of New York — its President Michael A. Cooper, Executive Director Barbara Berger Opotowsky, present and former Chairs and Secretary of the Committee on Women in the Profession Susan Kohlmann, Kathy Rodgers, and Melissa Sobel, and Committee Coordinator Martha Harris — in bringing this book and its ideas to the attention of the New York City legal community by co-sponsoring with the Foundation the conference "Growing and Keeping Talented Lawyers: New Directions in Mentoring" held January 24, 2000, at the Association's home.

We would also like to acknowledge: Barbara A. Ryan, President (1999-2000), the New York Women's Bar Association; Foundation President

(1999-2000) Nancy L. Lazar; Foundation Directors Toby J. Pilsner (also a Founder), Denise Coleman, Marilyn Kunstler, and Carol A. Schrager; Meryl R. Kaynard, Co-Chair of the Employment and Equal Opportunity Committee, New York Women's Bar Association; this project's first mentor, Sheila H. Akabas, Ph.D., Professor, Columbia University School of Social Work and Director of the School's Workplace Center, whose encouragement and confidence in us strengthened the Foundation to take on both this book and the mentoring conference; Robin Moss Henkin, M.S.W., formerly Professor Akabas' graduate student-protégé and now a social work professional, who elicited our first serious thinking about mentoring in the legal profession; Suzanne Baer, President of Baer Diversity Resources and formerly diversity consultant to corporate law firm members of the Committee to Enhance Opportunities for Minorities in the Profession and Assistant to the President for Minority Affairs of the Association of the Bar of the City of New York, who helped us see the close relationship between the challenges faced by women and minorities in the legal profession; Wendy H. Schwartz, who established the New York Women's Bar Association's group mentoring program and Elise A. Yablonski, who continues to administer it, for their dedication to the success of the project that inspired this book and the mentoring conference; the anonymous donor of seed money to the Foundation for a model mentoring project; our colleagues on the mentoring conference planning group — Ilene Knable Gotts, Kara L. Gross, Felicia Henderson, Joan F. Krey, Abby Sternschein Mendelsohn, Tamar Niv, Eva H. Posman, Erin Raccah, Mary V. Rosado, Tamara Stephen, and Iris Temple; and last but not least, Gina Anderson's husband Tom Anderson and daughter Erica, Meg Gifford's husband James Daniels, and Jolie Schwab's husband David Hodes and children Alex, Emily, and Spencer — without whose love and support our mentoring project would not exist.

G.S.A.

M.E.G.

J.E.S.

Acknowledgments

by the Author

Little did I know when Gina Anderson first called me just a year ago that she and I would be embarking on the journey that led to this book. She said that she and the New York Women's Bar Association Foundation were hoping to sponsor a conference on mentoring and asked if I would be interested in working with them. The offer — like Gina herself — was irresistible given my interest in mentoring and in the career advancement of women. Showing lawyers how to be mentors and enjoy the benefits of mentoring has been a large part of my consulting practice and of my law practice before that, and I welcomed the opportunity to be involved in the Foundation's conference. Gina also asked if I might draft "a little handbook" for distribution at that conference. That "little handbook" is what you are reading now.

I am greatly indebted to Gina. She has been an inspiration, a source of superb advice, and a pleasure to work with during our long distance collaboration. Her energy, dedication, and passion for this project have been unfailing. She has given and taught me a great deal, and I am very fortunate to have her support and friendship.

I thank the New York Women's Bar Association Foundation for sponsoring this book and providing encouragement and support to make it a reality. Dedicated to career support and advancement for women, the Foundation recognized that mentoring was important for all lawyers and invited me to help them spread the word through this book. Special thanks to Gina and to Jolie Schwab for reading the first draft and giving me excellent feedback; to Nancy Lazar and the technology support staff at Davis Polk & Wardwell for helping me overcome software communication hurdles; to Kara Gross and Dr. Sheila Akabas for their research assistance; and to the many other women I have met who prove the value of a strong, smart, and vibrant women's network.

Much of the interest in mentoring that led to this book was generated by the National Association for Law Placement (NALP) Foundation research report entitled *Keeping the Keepers: Strategies for Associate Retention in Times of Attrition*. I appreciate the opportunity NALP gave me to build on their work. Special thanks to Paula Patton, NALP Executive Director, and Janet Smith, NALP Director of Publications, for their assistance throughout the editing and publishing process.

Since its beginning, the Professional Development Consortium has been an important influence in my work. Its members are dedicated to helping lawyers and firms achieve their enormous potential through in-house training and development, including mentoring. I am proud and grateful to be a part of this fine organization.

Thanks to the many clients, colleagues, and friends who shared their mentoring stories with me and encouraged my quest to help lawyers find professional success and personal fulfillment.

Some of the thoughts in this book have appeared in my columns for *Law Firm Governance* and its predecessor, *Law Governance Review*. That journal has been most supportive in offering me a forum to present ideas about mentoring and other professional development practices.

My sons, Jordan and David, showed remarkable patience with me during the writing process, and their good humor (and surprise *dim sum*) made the most tedious periods easier to bear. I love being their mother and hope they always find the mentors they need and act as mentors to others.

Most importantly, my love and gratitude go to my husband, Myles, who worked with me every step of the way, and whose affection, attention to detail, sage advice, and sense of humor made this effort worthwhile. No one could be a better husband or mentor.

Ida Abbott

INTRODUCTION

"In the beginning is relation."

MARTIN BUBER, I AND THOU

Mentoring means different things to different people. For purposes of this book, a **mentor** is a person who helps a lawyer develop professionally to achieve the lawyer's desired professional goals, and **mentoring** is *the process by which the mentor and protégé work together to identify and help the protégé work toward those professional goals.* The terms are derived from the relationship between Mentor (an earthly incarnation of the goddess Athena) and Telemachus, Odysseus' son in Homer's *The Odyssey*.

Since these classical beginnings, mentoring has described a one-on-one relationship between an all-powerful elder teacher and a neophyte who is taught, nurtured, and protected. Today mentoring encompasses a range of different behaviors, takes many forms (from pairs to small groups to large structured programs), and involves mentors and protégés at all career stages. Protégés may have several mentors, and mentors may have several protégés — all at once or sequentially — each serving a different purpose.

Regardless of the form mentoring takes, when done correctly, it is a proven and cost-effective approach to many of the problems that face the legal profession. Mentoring helps individual lawyers develop professional excellence, which in turn provides the proficient, productive, and profitable lawyers needed to serve an employer's clients and ensure an institution's success and survival. Mentoring is powerful because it joins the interests of individual lawyers with those of the organization.

Most lawyers and legal employers recognize the importance of mentoring, so why isn't mentoring practiced widely and effectively in the legal profession? Lawyers were traditionally trained and prepared for practice through mentoring, but changed conditions make mentoring much less likely to occur naturally in today's legal work-place. Rapid law firm growth, increased competition, brutal time and work pressures, a turbulent job market, and spiraling attrition all work against the development and sustenance of traditional mentoring relationships. Yet this changed legal environment makes mentoring more sought after now than ever.

Young lawyers today strongly associate mentoring with professional development, career advancement, and longer-term commitment to an employer. This point is documented in two recent studies by the NALP Foundation for Research and Education, *Keeping the Keepers: Strategies for Associate Retention in Times of Attrition* (1998) and *Perceptions of Partnership: The Allure and Accessibility of the Brass Ring* (1999). These reports issue a warning that unless legal employers provide mentoring for their employees, the most talented lawyers will continue to depart for other legal employers, businesses, and professions.

This is a loss employers cannot afford. Soaring associate attrition is driving up law firm costs, creating staffing nightmares, straining client relations, and jeopardizing the future leadership of many law firms throughout the country. In response, many firms are using financial incentives to try to keep associates from leaving. While these work in the short term, what keeps lawyers over the long term is the satisfaction of professional growth, personal attention, and belonging to an organization that values them as individuals and wants to help them succeed. These are the benefits of mentoring.

Some employers have tried to remedy the decline in traditional mentoring by instituting formal mentoring programs. Mentoring programs can and do succeed, but only when their objectives are clear and limited, program elements are well planned and monitored, and lawyers are prepared, trained, and encouraged to participate. When an organization makes mentoring an integral part of its culture, the organization encourages all employees to be mentors for one another and sends a clear message about the sincerity of its commitment to the development of its employees. Such programs now exist in business, education, accounting, and other professions. They can work for lawyers, too.

The Lawyer's Guide to Mentoring shows how lawyers can have satisfying and effective mentoring relationships and how employers can institute programs that make those relationships available. This book describes how to use mentoring as a critical strategy for professional development, job satisfaction, and attorney retention. It demystifies the role of the mentor, explains why and how the protégé must be an active participant in the mentoring process, and shows readers how to make mentoring relationships flourish. *The Lawyer's Guide to Mentoring* offers pragmatic approaches that will enable readers to incorporate mentoring practices into daily work life. This book combines the best of traditional mentoring with the best recent mentoring innovations to produce a new model of mentoring for lawyers that is realistic, effective, and attainable.

HOW TO USE THIS BOOK

The Lawyer's Guide to Mentoring is directed to every lawyer interested in being a mentor or having one and to every employer who wishes to make mentoring available in the workplace. Chapters One to Four explore the dynamics of mentoring relationships and how mentoring can benefit lawyers and legal employers. Chapter Five describes how lawyers can start and maintain mentoring relationships, while Chapters Six through Eleven explain how to establish successful mentoring programs in the legal workplace. If your organization is thinking about starting a mentoring program, or if you have tried mentoring programs unsuccessfully in the past but would like to try again, the information and checklists provided will be of help. The discussion concentrates on the most common mentoring programs, those designed for associates with more senior attorneys acting as mentors. But other types of mentoring programs are also covered, including informal, group, and peer mentoring.

This book applies to lawyers at every stage of their careers and in every type of practice, and to all legal employers. For purposes of brevity, law firm terminology is used, but this is not intended to limit the general applicability of the mentoring principles and programs discussed. If you do not work in a law firm, I hope you will read these terms broadly and apply this book's lessons to your own situation.

Anecdotes about lawyers' mentoring experiences appear throughout the text. Unless otherwise specifically noted, they do not refer to real people but are illustrative stories and composites based on mentoring experiences related to me by hundreds of lawyers in the course of my consulting work. In every case, the names are pseudonyms.

CHAPTER 1

ADAPTING MENTORING TO THE MODERN LEGAL WORKPLACE

"Those having torches will pass them on to others."

PLATO, THE REPUBLIC

Mentoring has always existed in law firms. Traditionally, mentoring was a long-term, one-on-one relationship between an inexperienced protégé and a more experienced lawyer who acted as a teacher, guide, adviser, advocate and confidante. This relationship arose through a fortuitous combination of chance and chemistry. Two lawyers working together would find that they shared mutual professional interests and personal affinities. The senior attorney, seeing promise in the junior, invested time and effort to promote the protégé's career and bestowed upon the protégé the benefits of his power and influence. The mentor opened career doors for the protégé and escorted him into the boardrooms of power. Informal and unplanned, the relationship had no discernible starting point and evolved over time.

The legal workplace has changed, but lawyers' expectations for mentoring have not. When lawyers today are asked to explain what they mean by "mentor," the breadth of responses is stunning. Over the years, I have asked lawyers to answer the question, "What do mentors do?" *Table 1* shows how one focus group of lawyers responded to that question. Lawyers do not expect mentors to do just a few of the things listed in *Table 1*; they expect mentors to do *all* of these things. Is it any wonder that lawyers are reluctant to become mentors, or that associates' expectations are dashed when mentors perform only a few of these functions?

TABLE 1. ONE FOCUS GROUP'S RESPONSES TO THE QUESTION "WHAT DO MENTORS DO?"

- Teach
- Care
- Acknowledge
- Validate
- Explain
- Communicate
- Debrief
- Facilitate
- Inspire
- Be role models
- Appreciate
- Talk
- Introduce ideas, people, resources
- Use clout/influence
- Go to bat for you — protect and advocate
- Stay available, accessible
- Train
- Help
- Support
- Answer questions
- Provide friendship
- Help with career choices
- Teach the ropes
- Help you not reinvent the wheel
- Provide career opportunities — build client base
- Provide opportunities to observe
- Educate about practice, politics, personalities
- Console
- Navigate (help avoid pitfalls)
- Help you get out of a bad situation
- Give career guidance, long and short term
- Inform about the work being done
- Be someone safe to talk openly with
- Facilitate access to work opportunities
- Teach substantive skills
- Advocate for you to others
- Advise on longer-term career development
- Discuss professional issues
- Give feedback on work product
- Educate on areas not found in books
- Give practical experience
- Encourage
- Look for plum assignments for you
- Help you move upward
- Offer professional development ideas
- Dispense wisdom
- Teach strategy and technical skills
- Integrate work life/rest of life
- Trust
- Serve as a realistic sounding board
- Work with you
- Tell oral history, war stories
- Give vision of future
- Have empathy
- Have a personal connection
- Provide a different perspective

The new model of mentoring necessarily pares down these expectations. Contemporary mentoring continues to emphasize the mentor's roles and functions (*Table 2*), but individual mentors are no longer expected to perform all of these functions. A mentor may serve several of the traditional functions or only one. The new model departs from the traditional one in several other ways. (*Table 3.*) Most significantly, lawyers who want mentors no longer wait to be chosen. They decide what they want to learn and accomplish and who can help them achieve their goals and objectives, and then initiate, set goals for, and maintain mentoring relationships.

TABLE 2. ROLES AND FUNCTIONS OF MENTORS

Roles	Functions
Host	Welcomes protégés to the firm, introduces them to others
Bridge	Acts as a link to the firm for work, support, administrative information
Protector	Provides support, runs interference
Guide	Explains firm political issues and unwritten rules
Champion	Advocates for protégé's promotion within the firm
Social director	Helps individuals get involved in firm social affairs
Teacher	Teaches legal and practice skills
Role model	Demonstrates appropriate behaviors and attitudes
Coach	Provides feedback, monitors performance and experience, encourages professional growth, gives "stretch" assignments
Career counselor	Advises about work assignments, career decisions, professional dilemmas
Troubleshooter	Helps with problems
Sounding board	Listens to ideas, proposals, plans
Confidante	Listens to individuals express doubts and fears
Enhancer	Builds confidence
Business source	Connects individuals to networks, business contacts
Sponsor	Opens doors to business, community, outside opportunities
Publicist	Promotes individual outside the firm
Friend	Forms personal and social bonds
Catalyst	Makes things happen, inspires action, looks for new possibilities

Adapted from "Mentoring Plays a Key Role in Retaining Attorneys of Color" by Ida O. Abbott, Esq., *Law Governance Review*, Spring 1998.

TABLE 3. COMPARING OLD AND NEW MODELS OF MENTORING

Old model	New model
Mentor selects	Protégé initiates
One mentor	Many mentors
Mentor/protégé similarities	Differences valued
One-on-one only	Pairs or groups
General career-oriented	Specific, goal-oriented
Mentor teaches protégé	Reciprocal learning
For young lawyers	For all lawyers
Long-term	Variable terms
Hierarchical	Peers, juniors can be mentors
Mentor is a senior lawyer	Need not be a lawyer
Same organization	Inside or outside organization

Adapted from "Mentoring Plays a Key Role in Retaining Attorneys of Color" by Ida O. Abbott, Esq., *Law Governance Review*, Spring 1998.

Instead of aspiring to find a single perfect mentor, this new approach counsels lawyers to develop a network of relationships with many mentors at different times and for different developmental purposes: teaching a new lawyer the organization's unwritten rules, championing a senior associate for partnership, counseling an older partner about retirement. Lawyers may have numerous mentors at once, at different times, and for different purposes. Mentors can be men or women, older or younger, lawyers or not. Some will guide the protégé's career over several years, while others will have only brief or limited influence. Together, these mentors form a mentoring "board of advisors" that provides career resources and assistance to the protégé as needed.[1]

By redefining the scope of the mentoring relationship and the people who can serve as mentors, the new model increases lawyers' ability to find mentors. Potential mentors may be more willing to serve when they know that their obligations are clearly delimited. When the scope of a mentoring relationship is restricted, mentors need not

---

[1] Marshall Loeb, "The New Mentoring," *Fortune Magazine*, November 27, 1995, p. 213.

invest as much time in a single individual. They may work with one protégé at a time, or, through group mentoring, they can share their expertise, support, and influence with a larger number of protégés. Moreover, because they can concentrate on their particular areas of strength and interest, mentors can enjoy mentoring more.

The new model is an essential adaptation because the work conditions that gave rise to traditional mentoring relationships no longer exist. In the past, an apprenticeship system in law firms fostered the development of such relationships. This kind of mentoring was assisted by the homogeneity of the legal profession, which was comprised almost exclusively of white men, usually from similar backgrounds and schools. Partners could see themselves reflected in the young men around them and "clone" themselves through the mentoring process.

Things began to change in the 1970s. Law firms began to hire large numbers of associates, which made the traditional one-on-one apprenticeship model impractical. Law firms had to find a more systematic way to train these associates, so they implemented orientation and training programs that used seminars, lectures, panel presentations, and other methods more suitable for teaching associates in groups. Formal orientation and training programs replaced one-on-one relationships as the primary channels for associate development.

At about the same time, women and minority lawyers began to enter the profession in large numbers. Prior to the 1970s, more than 95 percent of law firm partners and associates were men. Between 1970 and 1980, the number of women graduating from law school rose more than 600 percent, from 6,700 to 41,000, and the number of minority graduates almost doubled, rising from 5,600 to 10,600. Unlike the white male associates from similar backgrounds to whom partners could easily relate, these new lawyers were virtual strangers to the legal profession and did not blend into the existing law firm culture. Partners found it uncomfortable and difficult to be mentors to these lawyers. Consequently, many women and minority lawyers remained "outsiders" until they left their firms — which happened frequently.

In response, law firms in the late 1970s and 1980s began to introduce formal mentoring programs designed to assimilate these female and minority "outsiders" into the dominant firm culture. But, because law firms had become highly impersonal organizations for all associates and little mentoring went on for anyone, most of these programs took a broader, more democratic approach and assigned mentors to all new lawyers, not just to women and minorities. These programs recognized the importance of individualized attention and assigned partners or senior associates to act as mentors for newly arrived associates. The mentor's role was to assist in the transition to legal practice and life in the firm. Mentors were expected to answer questions, teach new associates the ropes, and accompany them to firm-sponsored social events. Although well-intentioned, these programs were generally short-lived and rarely led to meaningful mentoring relationships.

The reasons these early programs failed are the same reasons mentoring programs fail today. Program goals tend to be vague and ill-defined, and programs are not monitored or evaluated. Many assigned mentors do not know how to be mentors or are not really interested in mentoring protégés they hardly know. Economic changes in law practice discourage non-billable activities such as mentoring and training. Bottom line pressures mean that lawyers are working longer hours to maximize revenues, develop business, and handle growing administrative responsibilities, while they are not rewarded in tangible ways for their mentoring efforts. High turnover and increased work demands make it hard to find the time for a mentoring relationship to take root, much less blossom. Most importantly, however, the trust, mutual respect, and affection that are the foundation of a genuine mentoring relationship cannot be imposed by a "mentoring committee." As a consequence, few mentoring programs have been effective, and most have been disappointing for the lawyers and for their firms.

The 1990s saw a reevaluation of law firm mentoring efforts. Mentoring relationships have become even harder to form today because of the accelerating changes in law practice: the growth and geographical expansion of law firms, the continuing increase in lawyer diversity, financial and competitive pressures, and high turnover. Nonetheless, in response to troubling news articles, exit interviews, and studies showing that associates leave law firms because they do not receive sufficient mentoring, firms are placing mentoring initiatives in the forefront of their strategies for recruitment and retention. The reason is mostly economic: attrition is costing firms a fortune, and slowing down the rate of associate departures is money in a firm's pocket. But firms also realize that mentoring is integral to associate training and development — and an effective way to help experienced lawyers deal with the pressures and challenges of contemporary practice.

CHAPTER 2

HOW MENTORING RELATIONSHIPS WORK

*"The greatest good you can do for another is not just
to share your riches but to reveal to him his own."*

BENJAMIN DISRAELI

Mentoring is a vigorous and dynamic process, not an event. It operates through personal relationships where learning takes place. Although most people think of a mentor's influence on the protégé, mentoring relationships are reciprocal, benefiting the mentor as well. Mentors contribute their knowledge and advice to help the protégé become a better lawyer, but the mentoring experience provides opportunities for the mentor to learn as well as teach. Protégés can offer their mentors new ideas, fresh perspectives, and expertise in areas outside the mentor's field.

Still, the focus of the mentoring process is on helping the protégé. The mentoring relationship is developmental and, ultimately, transformative as protégés learn new skills, develop greater confidence, and move toward optimizing their potential. As these changes occur, the protégé learns to think and act differently, with greater professional judgment and maturity. Some of these changes are simply a factor of increasing age and experience. But mentors influence the direction and quality of the protégé's development. They can help the natural maturation process take shape more easily, quickly, and fully, and with fewer unnecessary diversions.

The particular nature of mentoring relationships varies. If described along a continuum, at one end would be intense, paternalistic relationships where a mentor is deeply and personally involved in guiding and promoting the protégé's career. At the other end of the continuum are mentor-protégé relationships where the mentor is little more than a "buddy" or "pal" who checks in occasionally to see how the protégé is getting along. Along the continuum are relationships with many different levels of intensity and involvement in which the mentor serves many kinds of functions.

Whatever mentoring roles individual mentors assume, mentors in general serve two principal types of functions: career functions and psychosocial functions. In her seminal book, *Mentoring in the Workplace*, Kathy Kram, Director of the Executive MBA program at Boston University School of Management, identified these as the functions that differentiate mentoring relationships from other forms of work relationships. Career functions promote professional growth by coaching, providing needed information, and exercising organizational leverage to help a protégé advance. Psychosocial functions are those aspects of mentoring that build confidence, a clear sense of identity, and effectiveness in a professional role.

CAREER FUNCTIONS

For lawyers, the career function operates by virtue of the mentor's greater experience and more influential position in the organization. Based on a perception that the junior person is competent and shows potential, the mentor helps the protégé navigate and rise in the organization through sponsorship, challenging work assignments, coaching, and protection. The mentor helps the protégé understand how the firm operates and what the protégé has to do to advance. The protégé learns how to function effectively in the firm and the profession and prepares for career advancement.

Mentors sometimes help protégés learn good legal skills, but a large part of career success depends on more than technical ability. Professional development requires in large measure attitudes and aptitudes that are less concrete: self-confidence, professional judgment, intuition, and the ability to turn aspirations into achievements. Proficiencies in these areas come with experience and encouragement; mentors provide both. Mentors steer protégés to challenging work that will give them visibility and a chance to prove their mettle. Lawyers tend to be high performers with high career ambitions. They need to know how they are progressing, and they place a great deal of importance on feedback. Mentors can offer meaningful feedback, reinforce lessons learned from experience, and provide continued encouragement if their protégés experience setbacks. As a protégé becomes increasingly competent, confidence also grows. Career goals become easier to visualize and achieve.

The career function also links to career success by providing a special form of entry into informal social networks that offer many important advantages.[1] People who become part of key networks tend to be more committed to and successful in their organizations, while exclusion from these networks causes people to leave.[2] Through an organization's informal networks, protégés have access to valuable information that is not commonly available through normal communication channels, opportunities for exposure and visibility to high-level decision makers, and chances to build alliances and coalitions with influential people. Being able to acquire valuable information, display competence to senior partners, and get to know and work with these partners is likely to enhance career outcomes. At the same time, the mentor's career benefits from the relationship as the mentor develops protégés who will proficiently serve the mentor's clients and support the mentor's own practice and professional goals.

PSYCHOSOCIAL FUNCTIONS

In contrast to the mentor's career functions, which relate to the protégé's organizational role, psychosocial functions deal with the protégé's self-image and comfort in a professional role. Psychosocial functions depend to a large extent on the mutual trust, respect, and increasing intimacy which develop in an interpersonal relationship. Unlike the career function, which depends on the mentor's position and influence in the organization, the psychosocial mentoring function depends more on the quality of the relationship between mentor and protégé. As the two individuals interact, the mentor's acceptance and confirmation of the protégé strengthens the protégé's confidence and sense of self-worth. The mentor becomes a role model and counselor, helping the protégé deal with the dilemmas of practice and develop a personal style and professional identity. The relationship also has psychosocial benefits for the mentor by reinforcing the mentor's self-image as someone with valuable wisdom and experience worth sharing.

---

[1] See Catalyst, "Women in Corporate Leadership: Progress and Prospects," and Dreher in the References section at the conclusion of this book.

[2] Karen Stephenson, "Diversity: A Managerial Paradox," *Clinical Sociology Review*, 1994.

Within a mentoring relationship, the career and psychosocial functions interrelate and often overlap. When a mentor gives a protégé a tough but exciting new assignment, the protégé not only learns the new skills required for the task but also benefits psychologically from the mentor's confidence that the protégé was ready and able to take on the job. Likewise, when a protégé is having trouble working with another lawyer, the mentor may be supportive and at the same time advise the protégé about the practical and political realities of working with difficult people. The extent to which a mentoring relationship embraces career and psychosocial functions depends on the individuals' needs and interpersonal skills, the degree of trust in the relationship, and whether the organizational context provides sufficient opportunities and encouragement for mentoring activities.

INTERPERSONAL FACTORS

Mentoring relationships are shaped by the personal and interpersonal dynamics of the two people involved. Each individual brings a unique set of needs, interests, abilities, and concerns to a mentoring relationship, and the relationship changes over time as those factors change. At various stages of life and career, those factors determine what individuals bring to and seek from a mentoring relationship. At the beginning of a career, young lawyers focus on developing the skills, competence, and professional identity they need to establish themselves in law practice. New lawyers have questions and worries about their choice of career and employer, about whether partnership or advancement in the organization is desirable or achievable, and about the tensions between work demands and personal life. They seek relationships with more experienced mentors who can help them work on these developmental concerns.

Experienced lawyers also need mentors, especially when they reach transition points in their own careers. A lawyer in mid-career has established competence and professional identity but may be considering a redirection in practice area, employment, or profession. Mid-career lawyers look back on what they have accomplished and ahead to what will be required for them to continue along the career path they have chosen. Senior lawyers not only face these same concerns but also must come to terms with increasing changes in practice and technology at a time when their interest and energy may be declining. As a result of reflection and reassessment, these lawyers may experience renewed commitment to practice and periods of increased creativity, or they may suffer self-doubt and fear that career options are becoming more limited and time is running out. In either case, mid-career and senior lawyers may look to peers or to more experienced mentors for guidance, support, and advice.

ORGANIZATIONAL CULTURE

When mentoring takes place at work, the relationship is strongly influenced by the organizational context. Organizational factors that affect the frequency and quality of workplace mentoring include the degree of hierarchy and internal competition, the performance appraisal and reward systems, and the emphasis placed by the firm on professional development and work satisfaction. In order to thrive, mentoring requires a culture that values and rewards professional development, collaboration, and concern for others. A law firm where little attention is given to professional development, where associates are afraid of partners (or some partners are afraid of other partners), where partners compete against each other for business and recognition, and where the bottom line is all that matters, will not sustain healthy mentoring relationships.

MEANINGFUL MENTORING RELATIONSHIPS

The best mentoring relationships develop when both protégés and mentors approach the relationship with positive attitudes. For the protégé, this means being receptive to the mentoring process. This is not always as easy as it sounds. Working with a mentor means facing up to feelings of inadequacy, self-doubt, or insecurity, which can be very threatening. Most young lawyers have enjoyed repeated success and achievement in school and other experiences leading up to law practice. They are given large salaries and responsibilities, and are expected to perform at a very lofty professional level. Admitting the need for help makes some of these lawyers feel vulnerable; therefore, they do not take advantage of the mentor's offer of help. This continues to be a problem for some lawyers as they become established and successful — and even less willing to accept a mentor's help. In addition, protégés may have career-related fears they are afraid to face; they may have competing priorities for their time; they may view the mentoring relationship as insignificant; or they may feel guilty about taking the time of overworked mentors who have their own troubles to deal with. Protégés who overcome these concerns and are willing to accept the helping hand that mentors extend will find that mentors can be of enormous value. By being open and receptive to their mentors' assistance, protégés will derive maximum benefit from a mentoring relationship.

Being a mentor is a privilege and a responsibility. Because they impact lawyers' psyches as well their careers, mentors can wield enormous power. Mentors influence the way young lawyers see themselves and how their professional identities evolve. By getting their protégés appointed to key committees, suggesting them for visible assignments, and sponsoring them for partnership or promotion, mentors take concrete steps to build self-esteem and advance their protégés in the organization. That is why a mentor's approval is so coveted and why a mentor's criticism can be so devastating. That is also why mentors have to be sensitive to wield their influence responsibly for the protégé's benefit.

The sine qua non of being an effective mentor is caring about another person's success. Mentoring requires a generosity of spirit. It presupposes a willingness to go out of one's way to help others achieve goals that are important to them. Individuals who are preoccupied with their own needs and goals, or who do not really care about other people, do not make good mentors. The best mentors are those who truly believe in the importance of mentoring and are dedicated to helping other people achieve their goals.

But caring about a lawyer's development does not mean mentors take a personal interest in every young lawyer who views them as a mentor. Most mentors prefer to work with protégés who quickly demonstrate a mastery of law practice and show great promise. Not all junior lawyers demonstrate such promise, at least not right away. Frequently, those who need mentoring most are those who need some time, attention, and experience before they bloom. Mentors need patience. They must be willing to give protégés regular coaching and repeated opportunities (coupled with copious feedback) to prove they can excel.

CHAPTER 3

THE BENEFITS OF MENTORING

"Those who seek mentoring will rule
the great expanse under heaven."

SHU CHING

The strong link between mentoring relationships and career success is well established. Successful business executives and lawyers consistently point to mentoring as important to their success and to a lack of mentors as an impediment to career advancement. This has been documented in several studies over more than two decades by the NALP Foundation, by Catalyst (a research organization specializing in women in the workplace), and by other organizations that study career patterns and success factors. In a 1986 survey by Korn/Ferry, a large executive search firm, executives rated mentoring second only to education as a significant factor in achieving success. Research shows that employees who have mentors report feeling more in tune with their firm's way of thinking and doing things, more nurtured and supported during the promotion process, and more aware of firm politics.[1] Studies that measure the outcomes of mentoring have found that protégés enjoy benefits that are both intangible (e.g., recognition, job satisfaction) and tangible (e.g., increased compensation, promotions).[2] These studies also confirm that a mentor's coaching and support motivate protégés to strive for excellence and success.

Mentoring is a key driver of work satisfaction and employee retention.[3] Several recent surveys have confirmed that people who feel they

---

[1] See Dreher, Scandura, and Chao in the References at the conclusion of this book.
[2] See Scandura and Dreher.
[3] See Scandura.

do not have enough opportunities for mentoring are significantly more likely to leave their jobs. A national "Emerging Work Force Study" conducted by Interim Services, Inc., and Louis Harris and Associates in 1999 found that 61 percent of employees who think their employers provide them with mentoring opportunities say they are likely to stay in their jobs for the next five years. In contrast, employees stated that lack of mentoring opportunities makes them twice as likely to look for another job within the next year. Similarly, the Hay Group, a large human resources consulting firm, surveyed half a million employees at more than 300 companies to determine the factors that affect retention. This 1998 survey compared the attitudes of employees who said they would stay with their company for more than five years with those who said they planned to leave within a year. Of more than 50 factors analyzed in the survey, the opportunity to learn and use new skills and the availability of coaching and feedback — both significant elements of mentoring — ranked within the top five employee retention factors. (Compensation, incidentally, was one of the least important factors.)

Today's lawyers place a great deal of importance on having mentors who can help them develop the self-confidence, institutional savvy, legal skills, and professional connections they need to achieve their goals and ambitions. In studies and surveys of lawyer dissatisfaction and law firm attrition, associates repeatedly point to the lack of mentoring as a principal reason for leaving their firms (e.g., NALP Foundation, *Keeping the Keepers*). Talented associates want to excel, and they work very, very hard. They understand that they cannot depend on their law firms for tenure but must rely on their own wits and abilities. In return for their intelligence and hard work, they expect their employers to help them acquire the skills and knowledge they need to succeed in their firms or elsewhere.

Mentoring is a highly effective way to give associates the practical training, development opportunities, and personal attention they need. Being a lawyer involves far more than exercising a set of technical skills. Even the brightest and most successful law students know little about the *practice* of law when they graduate. Lawyers learn most of what they need to know as practitioners while they are out in the workplace. As the NALP Foundation study *Keeping the Keepers* noted, "Associates crave exposure to role models who provide everyday opportunities to work through issues in a case or develop a strategy for handling a matter. Allowing an associate to shadow a receptive partner is far more meaningful than any CLE program" (p. 40). This need to grow and develop continues throughout a lawyer's career. In order to continue advancing in a firm or in the legal community — and to keep up with changes in the law and the legal services marketplace — lawyers must be continually learning and adapting.

Mentoring is powerful because a mentor communicates implicitly, "I am interested in you as a person. I want you to succeed." Mentoring is a *personal* relationship based on mutual regard. It addresses the elemental need all of us have to be valued and appreciated for who we are, not the number of hours we bill. The pace and pressure of everyday life in the office leave many lawyers wondering whether anyone notices, much less cares about them. This insecurity, isolation, and alienation are particularly stark for lawyers new to practice or new to an office or firm. Having been wooed during the recruitment process, new lawyers enter an environment where they are put to work and otherwise ignored. Personal interaction is minimized, and organized social events seem forced. Under these conditions, having a mentor can make the difference between a lawyer who goes through the motions of practice and one who is really engaged, inspired, and on the road to success. The impact of a mentoring relationship can be intensely emotional and validating. As one attorney said of her mentor, "He makes me feel important. He sets me up to succeed."

BENEFITS OF MENTORING TO LEGAL EMPLOYERS

Mentoring produces many important benefits for legal employers. For example, mentoring:

- Aids recruitment;
- Boosts retention;
- Efficiently translates knowledge into practice;
- Passes on the firm's accumulated wisdom;
- Raises productivity;
- Builds and transmits firm culture;
- Promotes workforce diversity;
- Helps the organization adapt to change;

- Builds loyalty;
- Develops new leaders; and
- Overcomes workplace alienation.

Let's examine these benefits in detail.

■ AIDING RECRUITMENT

The market for legal talent is more competitive than ever before. Law firms are facing the smallest pool of law firm graduates in a decade, and the demand for those new lawyers — in business, technology, investment banking, consulting, and many other fields besides law — is unprecedented. According to recruitment data collected by NALP, larger law firms achieved a yield (i.e., the ratio of offers accepted to those made) of less than 30 percent during the 1998 fall recruitment season. In some areas, the yield was as low as 25 percent. This rate was much lower than expected, since many firms had historically enjoyed yields of 60 to 80 percent. These pressures are forcing law firms to find innovative strategies that make them attractive to prospective associates.

The *Keeping the Keepers* study showed that the availability of mentoring is a factor associates consider in deciding to join a law firm. Employers who can demonstrate their commitment to career development have a significant recruiting advantage over their competitors. Timothy Butler and James Waldroop, directors of the career development program at Harvard Business School, found that the single most important factor on the minds of new MBAs is not money but "whether a position will move their long-term careers in a chosen direction." In deciding which job to choose, students cited as a key factor the emphasis placed by a firm on its commitment to the development of its professionals. This is consistent with the importance new lawyers place on working in firms that make associate development a priority.

A firm with a reputation for being a good place to learn and grow professionally will find it easier to recruit new attorneys at every level. Legal papers, magazines, book publishers, and even law students, conduct frequent surveys about culture, work conditions, and job satisfaction in law firms. The results are published in various print and electronic media, including on-line chat rooms. Law students learn the "inside scoop" about a law firm by talking with associates who work there and with law students who worked in its summer program. As a result, law students and lateral attorneys have access to a huge amount of information about law firms from sources other than the firms themselves. They find out quickly whether or not a firm's recruiting materials honestly and accurately portray the training and mentoring provided. Law students will avoid firms that do not deliver good training and mentoring and look favorably upon firms that demonstrate their commitment to associate development. Associates who experience salutary mentoring relationships can be a firm's best recruiters.

■ BOOSTING RETENTION

Recruiting is only the first challenge. Law firms are struggling to retain the lawyers they hire, and associate attrition is one of the most serious problems faced by law firms today. The NALP Foundation's *Keeping the Keepers* study revealed that 9.2 percent of new associates leave their firms in the first year of employment, 26.5 percent leave before the end of the second year, and 43 percent leave before the end of the third year. Attrition rates are 3 to 7 percent higher for women and minorities, and even higher for minority women. At the end of five years, only one-third of associates are still at the same firm they started with. It has been estimated that a new associate in a large firm will see 300 other associates come and go by the time he or she becomes an equity partner.[1]

Having an influential mentor has a direct impact on an associate's decision to remain in a firm. Attorneys who believe that their firm cares about their professional development and success are less likely to leave. Through individual attention to associate development, mentoring complements formal training programs and creates an environment where coaching and learning are ongoing. The effect is to reinforce the firm's commitment to professional development, which results in less turnover, which translates into a greater return on the firm's investment in recruiting. When I recently asked one new law firm partner why he had stayed in his firm, he replied: "Frankly, when I started here I didn't think I would stay long. But the partner I worked with kept giving me positive feedback. He noticed my work and praised me to

---

[1] *Facing the Grail: Confronting the Cost of Work-Family Imbalance*, Boston Bar Association, 1999.

other partners. It made me feel good about myself and about the firm." Compare this to how Richard, a departing associate, was treated at his former firm: "After three months of working together, this partner still called me Robert. He never talked to me except to tell me what to do; after I did it, I never heard back from him. I wonder if he'll even notice that I've gone." Unfortunately, Richard's experience is not uncommon.

Law firms try to keep lawyers by increasing compensation, but financial incentives alone are insufficient. The power of money cannot be denied, especially when the sums are tens of thousands of dollars in "staying bonuses." These are the bonuses some large firms are paying to lawyers simply for staying at their firms for four, five, or more years. For these firms, the cost of attrition is so enormous that paying as much as $50,000 to keep a mid-level associate for an extra year or two is worthwhile.

Mentoring is a far less costly way to achieve the same end. It may not seem to have the same allure as cash, but, contrary to popular belief, associates want more from their work than money. It is true that associates who believe they are not fairly compensated will leave as soon as other opportunities present themselves. And it is understandably hard for attorneys in small firms and government agencies to resist an offer from another employer that increases their compensation by 50 percent or more. In addition, if work conditions are unsatisfactory, compensation — regardless of the level — will not keep disgruntled associates at their firms when they have opportunities to leave. But it is well established that what keeps people motivated and in their jobs over time are not monetary incentives but intrinsic rewards: mentoring, recognition, appreciation, challenging work, and a sense that their contributions are valued.[1] So long as compensation is seen as fair and competitive with market rates, most associates prefer to work in a collegial environment with people they like and respect.

This is why mentoring can be so effective in holding on to talented lawyers. Through attention and caring, mentors let lawyers know they are valued. Many lawyers (including partners) who leave law firms are surprised to hear that their partners and colleagues are sorry to see them go. Departing lawyers frequently describe the same reaction:

---

[1] Frederick Herzberg, "One More Time: How Do You Motivate Employees", *Harvard Business Review*, September-October, 1987; and "1999 Emerging Work Force Study," Interim Services Inc. and Louis Harris Associates.

"The first time anyone ever told me that I was valued was when I announced I was leaving." To the contrary, mid-level and senior associates who have been at the same firm since they started practice are invariably able to point to one or more lawyers in the firm who have taken an interest in them, explained things to them about the substance and process of law practice, and made them feel important.

■ EFFICIENTLY TRANSLATING KNOWLEDGE INTO PRACTICE

Law firms spend a fortune to recruit new associates and then pay associates enormous salaries while still having to train them to practice law. Because of the large investment firms have made in these lawyers, it is critical that associates become proficient and profitable as quickly as possible. Moreover, for client service, risk management, and quality control purposes, firms have to ensure that all of their junior lawyers are practicing according to the standards of the firm and the profession. The only way legal organizations can ensure that these lawyers are developing and practicing as they should is for experienced lawyers to personally train and mentor them.

Law schools are designed to teach students the intellectual discipline of law: legal principles, interpretation and analysis, approaches to problem solving. In order to become effective practitioners, new lawyers must be able to apply what they learn to real problems of real clients. Those who have had clinical courses or clerkships during law school may come to their firms with a taste of what the practice of law is like, but their experience is limited and rarely as stressful or complicated as what they will face in full-time practice. You don't learn to drive a car by reading an instruction book or attending a seminar. You have to get behind the wheel, maneuver through traffic, and learn to watch out for other drivers. Learning begins under the watchful eye of a driving instructor, who cautions you, guides you, and gradually lets you go. In the same way, young attorneys can acquire insight and judgment under the tutelage of an experienced lawyer-mentor who guides them through repeated and intense exposure to real and complex legal problems.

New attorneys must learn how law is practiced and how and why the legal process works as it does. They must develop good professional judgment and become confident practitioners. Although some of this can be taught through in-house workshops and seminars, real understanding and good professional judgment come with time, experience, and reflection. In a transactional practice, junior associates may be able to proofread documents to make sure that their contents are accurate and consistent, but without experience and guidance, these associates may not be able to judge whether any key terms are *omitted*. That requires the associate to understand why partners and clients decide to include some terms and leave others out, and what factors need to be considered when making those decisions. That learning, which is essential to the development of legal and business judgment, is facilitated when a mentor invites an associate to a meeting with the client, or takes some time to explain how and why decisions are made in negotiating a transaction. The information may be presented in a lecture, but in that format information remains abstract. When the associate learns while actually working on a deal, information and experience mesh. The lessons are more meaningful and memorable because they are real.

■ PASSING ON THE FIRM'S ACCUMULATED WISDOM

Within any legal organization, there is a wealth of accumulated knowledge and wisdom. Mentors are the repositories of this knowledge and wisdom, and pass it down from one generation of lawyers to the next. In doing so, mentors carry out the important obligation of the firm to provide institutional continuity. Mentors do this in many ways: by telling stories, sharing lessons they have learned, and teaching seminars. They also do it in the natural course of working closely with other lawyers in the firm over time. But many only engage in this type of mentoring activity if the firm makes it a priority. Firms that neglect this responsibility are doomed to inefficiency, dissipation, and loss. As one associate commented in her exit interview: "There is so much knowledge in this firm that is wasted because truly brilliant people don't spend enough time briefing their associates on the issues, the law, or the structure of the deal."

■ RAISING PRODUCTIVITY

There is convincing evidence in corporate America that mentoring yields higher productivity and performance from both mentors and their protégés.[1] Mentors who train and supervise their protégés know the protégés' capabilities and can count on them to follow through. When protégés have a better understanding of their work and have the necessary skills to do the work, mentors can delegate tasks with confidence. When protégés observe their mentors' discipline and hard work, they emulate the behavior. Their motivation to do superior work rises when they work with a mentor who cares about them. And when the mentor and protégé work together on client matters, the mentor can have a positive impact on the protégé's performance by setting standards, assigning projects, and giving feedback designed to meet both client needs and specific mentoring objectives.

■ BUILDING AND TRANSMITTING FIRM CULTURE

Resilient firms have a strong culture that binds people together. Mentors transmit that culture. When senior lawyers mentor their protégés, they relay and preserve what is special and valued about the organization. Firms emphasize their uniqueness in their recruiting efforts but then do little to ensure that their new lawyers — including laterals — embrace the firm's culture and values. Some law firms try to instill these in new associates during orientation by having senior partners talk about the history and achievements of the firm, but many new lawyers find the firm's history irrelevant. Lawyers really absorb the culture and values of a firm in the course of their daily work and interactions with others in the firm. A mentor who makes time for new lawyers and acts as a role model is far more influential than any oral presentation or written statement of values.

Moreover, people who are mentored are more likely to become mentors themselves. When mentoring becomes the organization's accepted and expected norm of behavior, the organization's culture will reflect the best qualities of its mentors: generosity, support and caring for colleagues, constant learning, encouraging others to stretch and excel, and promoting success all around. An environment of this type will attract and keep the finest lawyers and make everyone in the firm happy to be there.

---

[1] See Murray and Scandura in the References at the conclusion of this book.

■ FOSTERING CHANGE AND ADAPTABILITY

Because it promotes communication and information sharing, mentoring can be a catalyst for fostering healthy cultural change. Mentors can learn a lot from protégés about new trends and developments in law and business, and about issues and concerns of junior lawyers. The organization stays better informed and can move swiftly to address potential problems. When the firm contemplates making significant changes in firm policies or strategic direction, it can apprise protégés in advance and seek their feedback. Soliciting their input as part of the decision-making process reduces resistance and enables protégés to understand and accept the decisions that are made. Junior lawyers tend to be suspicious of management and are more likely to trust their mentors than other representatives of the organization.

By providing "safe havens" where mentors and protégés can try out innovative ideas and approaches, mentoring relationships promote creative change. Mentors and protégés can use each other as sounding boards. For example, a senior associate who wants to go off partnership track might work with a mentor to explore alternative career paths and strategize about how to present the associate's request to the partnership in the most persuasive way. In the process, they may develop some ideas about how the firm can use various non-traditional career paths (e.g., staff attorneys, counsel positions) to further its retention efforts.

■ PROMOTING WORKFORCE DIVERSITY

Law firms that do not attract and retain a diverse work force will find themselves at a competitive disadvantage in the legal marketplace of the future. In 1997, women and minorities represented 63 percent of all law school graduates,[1] and by 2005, women and minorities will account for nearly two-thirds of the country's total work force. Without fully integrating women and minorities into the legal work force, employers cannot properly serve their clients, including major corporations whose own employees and customer bases are increasingly global and diverse. These clients are demanding the same from their lawyers.

---

[1] Patricia W. Bass, "Law School Enrollment and Employment for Women and People of Color," *Diversity & the Bar*, Minority Corporate Counsel Association, August 1999.

Law firms that attract and retain women and minority attorneys are winning over clients and business, and many clients are awarding work to firms on the condition that women and minority attorneys are assigned to their matters. Firms that have proven their commitment to diversity will continue to attract women and minority attorneys as they become known as places where these lawyers are welcomed, valued, and promoted. Many majority lawyers also place great importance on a firm's commitment to diversity and shun employers with poor records in hiring and retaining minority lawyers. Firms that lag behind in diversity efforts will therefore suffer in recruiting as well as business.

Mentoring is a vital element of a legal employer's diversity efforts. When lawyers get to know each other through the mentoring process, stereotypes and preconceptions disappear and authentic relationships emerge. Mentoring creates cross-gender and cross-cultural relationships that break down social barriers and enable women and minority lawyers to feel and be accepted. Through these relationships, mentoring engenders personal and professional ties which will enhance the firm's ability to retain women and minority attorneys.

■ BUILDING LOYALTY

The meaning of loyalty is being redefined in the workplace. Lawyers used to view law firms as places where, through hard work and dedication, they became partners and enjoyed lifetime tenure. Once they became partners, lawyers rarely left their firms. Associates today cannot even imagine that model. What they see is a world where few associates become partners and where even "tenured" partners are given the boot. Law firm associates distrust the very notion of longevity at a single firm, and only 56 percent of all associates in law firms are interested in becoming partners according to the NALP Foundation's *Perceptions of Partnership*. In a world that is constantly changing and offers no guarantees, young lawyers do not want to sit still. To them, moving from firm to firm, or from law to another field of work, is the norm. Their attitude about loyalty is calculated and short-term: "I will work hard and with dedication on my assignments while I am here, so long as the firm gives me training, attention, challenging work, and opportunities to learn and grow."

Law firms have to show these lawyers why they should stay in their firms, and the best people to do that are mentors. Mentors can help associates adopt a long-term perspective by helping them to think about their firm as a place to have a career, not just a job. Mentors who are generous with their time, attention, and career assistance promote loyalty. Kelly, a new partner in a Los Angeles firm, tells of how her mentor, John, secured her loyalty and kept her at the firm. When the firm opened a Silicon Valley office, the managing partner asked Kelly, who was then an associate, to move there. Before Kelly left Los Angeles, John gave her a list of his contacts in the Bay Area and told her, "Go for it! This is all potential business for the firm. See if you can get it." Not only did Kelly bring in some business from these contacts, she learned that John had given her all the business origination credit. John's generosity and his confidence in Kelly eventually turned a promising associate into a grateful, loyal, and successful partner.

Compare Kelly's experience to that of Barton, a lawyer who discovered that his principal competitor for a large piece of business was his own partner in another city. Barton learned that he and his partner had both been trying to woo the same potential client for several months. When Barton suggested that the two of them combine their efforts and approach the potential client together, the partner rebuffed him and insisted that the client — and all the credit — "are mine alone. You eat what you kill." In fact, the client selected Barton as its lawyer. Shortly thereafter, unable to stomach the growing environment of vicious competition among his own partners, Barton left the firm and took the client with him.

■ DEVELOPING NEW LEADERS

To ensure the future success of the firm, today's law firm leaders must nurture leadership skills and talents in the people who will follow them. Although firms can provide training in leadership skills and behaviors, not everyone can be taught to be a leader. Mentoring keeps partners in touch with their pool of potential leaders. Natural leaders will eventually emerge, but firms can create environments in which these people are identified and groomed at an early stage in their careers. When partners consciously identify their potential leaders, the firm can do more effective succession planning, allowing these potential new leaders to come forward and preparing them to assume leadership roles.

A close relationship with a respected mentor is likely to keep a potential leader stretching for growth and achievement. Mentors can challenge promising lawyers to fulfill their potential by placing them in situations that require them to draw on their leadership talents and by helping them to appreciate the meaning of those experiences. Most importantly, good mentors provide a safety net enabling future leaders to experiment and take risks within the firm. With this kind of support, potential leaders are more willing and able to assume leadership roles.

Penny is the first woman to be elected managing partner of her 80-lawyer firm. As an associate, she worked with a highly regarded litigation partner. One day, as they prepared for a client meeting to discuss strategy for an upcoming trial, the partner turned to her and said, "Penny, I'm going to tell the client that you will be the lead counsel at trial. You know this case better than anyone. And I know you're ready to do it." Penny did not feel ready but was eager for the chance. The client initially resisted, but the partner extolled Penny's abilities, explained why she should take the leading trial role, and then let her take center stage for the rest of the client meeting. Penny made such a favorable impression on the client that she overcame his doubts — and her own. She attributes her climb to leadership in the firm to her mentor's faith in her and, in particular, his willingness to give her leadership responsibility in that case.

■ OVERCOMING WORKPLACE ALIENATION

The conditions of law practice today are demoralizing and damaging for too many lawyers. This is evident not just from frequent job changes and the high number of lawyers leaving the profession altogether, but also from the elevated rates of stress and job dissatisfaction among lawyers and the alarming displays of incivility throughout the profession. Many of these problems are related to feelings of alienation and loneliness. These problems are especially acute for minority attorneys and women attorneys when their numbers in the firm or organization are low. Much of lawyers' work is solitary and cerebral, and lawyers often work independently. Alone, they can be productive and learn many technical skills. But most lawyers, even solo practitioners, find that constantly working alone becomes isolating, lonely, and professionally limiting.

Lawyers need more than just the intellectual challenge of law. Most people have a need for affiliation and acceptance in the workplace. Lawyers need to interact with others, to share ideas and personal concerns, and to feel part of something larger than themselves, whether it is the client team, the organization, or the legal profession. People need to connect with other people at work. They want to believe in the work they do and to work with other lawyers they like and respect. But, more and more, lawyers dislike their work environment and are so pressured by the demands of business that they lose touch with their colleagues, even those they see in the office every day. These conditions take a toll on the quality and productivity of their efforts.

Technology is compounding the problem. While technology has made many aspects of law practice more efficient, productive, and far-reaching, it has also eliminated the need for most face-to-face communication. Email, teleconferencing, video-conferencing, and on-line training programs have significantly reduced face-to-face interactions among lawyers. It is not uncommon to find lawyers sequestered in their offices, hardly speaking to anyone in person all day. Edward Hallowell, a Boston psychiatrist who teaches at Harvard Medical School, warns that replacing face-to-face interactions with technology results in the loss of the "human moment" — i.e., an authentic psychological encounter that can happen only when two people are in the same physical space and have each other's emotional and intellectual attention. Hallowell cautions that the loss of the human moment is causing widespread alienation and dysfunction in the workplace. He points out that people need human interaction to maintain their mental acuity and their emotional well-being. Hallowell does not argue that we should get rid of electronics but rather that we need to restore the human moment in the workplace. Mentoring is an effective way to do just that.

BENEFITS OF MENTORING FOR EXPERIENCED LAWYERS

Mentoring can benefit mid-career and senior lawyers as well as entry-level attorneys. Mentoring can:

- Help lawyers redefine professional identity during career transitions;
- Help lateral lawyers adapt to a new work environment more quickly and easily;
- Teach lateral lawyers how the new organization really operates (the "unwritten rules");

- Help lateral lawyers become oriented and integrated;

- "Market" lateral lawyers to other lawyers in the firm and to clients;

- Provide advice about contemplated career or practice changes; and

- Keep experienced lawyers marketable.

The benefits of mentoring for lawyers entering law practice are well known and appreciated, but mentoring is not limited to new lawyers. Mentors are valuable at every stage of a lawyer's career. Lawyers go through many changes, moves, and transitions over the decades they are in practice. At each career transition point, they face new challenges and undertake new responsibilities for which they may feel unprepared. One of the most common career transitions occurs with election to partnership. New partners redefine their professional identities as they begin to see themselves as owners and leaders rather than employees of the firm. New partners also find that the firm expects them to possess management, marketing, and business skills which they may not have, and this may make them uncomfortable. Eventually, new partners will learn what they need to know to make the transition, but a mentor can help them adapt more thoroughly, more quickly, and with less pain.

Mentors are also important for lawyers who move to another firm or organization. Employers assume that a lawyer who has practiced law elsewhere can "hit the ground running." They give little attention to helping the lateral attorney fit in socially, feel comfortable personally, and learn how things actually get done in this new environment. Take the example of the lawyers in one small California state agency. The four agency lawyers worked together well and were experts in their field. Because of a hiring freeze, they had not hired anyone for several years. When they were finally able to hire two additional lawyers, they put the new hires right to work and kept them very busy. But these new lawyers were struggling. They had experience practicing in the relevant fields of law but not in this particular office doing this kind of work. They floundered, afraid they would look incompetent if they asked questions, and reluctant to seek help from the four senior lawyers who formed a sort of closed "inner circle." When one of the senior lawyers realized that these new lawyers were feeling excluded and adrift, she started a mentoring effort within this small group. The four senior lawyers now take turns being mentors to the others. This mentoring effort has become more firmly established as the agency has continued to grow.

The adjustment process for laterals may involve reconciling expectations and realities. Associates in two firms which have very similar law practices may have extremely different work experiences. At Firm A, third-year litigation associates take depositions and have substantial responsibility for managing cases. Firm A may assume that all third-year lateral hires have similar experience while, in fact, third-year associates at Firm B do only written discovery and draft motions. When associates from Firm B arrive at Firm A, they are unprepared for the work they are given, which may lead to poor work experiences. A mentor can smooth the differences between the lateral associates' experience and the firm's expectations, and can help these associates develop the skills necessary to catch up to their peers in their new firm. Similarly, lateral associates sometimes bring assumptions and behaviors to their new employers that need to be corrected (e.g., the way legal secretaries are treated). Mentors can help laterals adjust their expectations and "unlearn" old habits that conflict with the new firm's culture.

Although associate attrition receives more attention, turnover among partners is also common today, with some partners moving many times from one law firm to another. A mentor can make the difference between a new partner's successful transition and a very short stay in the firm. A 1997 survey of satisfaction levels among 1,200 lateral partners by the international recruiting firm Major, Hagen & Africa found that one of the key indicators of lateral partner satisfaction was being effectively integrated into the partnership and culture of the firm, not just its business. Mentors can help lateral partners become oriented to the firm and begin to develop personal relationships that foster this integration. When joining a new firm, partners need to find ways to connect what they want to do with what the firm needs to have done. Other lawyers in the firm must understand what these lateral partners bring to the firm, what they hope to accomplish, and how they can help the firm. This process is also important for facilitating introductions to clients and integrating the partner into the firm's business development efforts. A mentor can expedite this internal marketing process.

Mentors can also assist experienced lawyers who contemplate changing legal fields, leaving a current employer, or leaving law practice altogether. Sometimes lawyers want to make a change because they develop a new interest or need a new challenge, but many lawyers are forced to change by external circumstances. In spite of the opportunities that abound in today's legal market, there is little job security, even for partners and senior counsel. Prosperous firms close, thriving practice areas dry up, and corporate jobs are eliminated. It is therefore crucial for all lawyers to remain "marketable" — i.e., to continually acquire the knowledge, hone the skills, and build the client base and professional networks they need to take control over the direction of their careers. This is important for all lawyers, because it is hard to predict when you may be confronted by a need to change, and the later in one's career, the more difficult it can be to make a significant career move. Having a mentor means that you do not have to face the change alone. Frank, for instance, had been a successful insurance defense lawyer for 25 years when his practice started to become less and less profitable. He sought advice from one of his partners who had left the litigation group several years earlier to start the firm's employment law practice. This partner met with Frank several times and counseled him about the issues and considerations involved in changing practice areas. With this mentor's help, Frank formed a clear picture of the practice area he wanted to develop and the firm agreed to support his efforts. Frank then formed a peer mentoring group with three other lawyers in the firm who were interested in making the change with him. Together, they studied the law and the market, created a business plan, and helped each other face the risks and uncertainties of their undertaking.

BENEFITS TO MENTORS

Mentoring also benefits mentors by helping them to:

- Attract and retain the best associates;
- Boost their own productivity;
- Increase profitability;
- Serve clients better;
- Free the mentor's time as protégés gain skills;
- Improve the mentor's performance;
- Further the mentor's professional development;

- Improve the mentor's management and communication skills;
- Enhance the mentor's leadership;
- Enhance the mentor's reputation;
- Advance the mentor's career;
- Expand their professional networks;
- Stay adaptable;
- Renew the mentor's sense of purpose;
- Prepare for personal changes;
- Feel personal satisfaction;
- Enhance their self-respect;
- Counteract isolation;
- Honor their own mentors;
- Leave a legacy; and
- Fulfill obligations to the legal profession.

The primary motivation for being a mentor is the natural human desire to share knowledge and experience in order to help another person develop. But not all mentoring is done for altruistic reasons; mentoring also promotes the mentor's self-interest. Mentoring is a smart management practice that contributes greatly to the mentor's success and makes the mentor's work life easier and more fulfilling.

Because most associates prefer to work with people who give them training and pay attention to their development needs, good mentors will be able to recruit — and keep — high caliber lawyers. Especially when associates are in short supply, good mentors can attract the best associates to staff their cases and serve their clients. And, since mentoring accelerates professional development and productivity, associates who are mentored serve clients more competently and efficiently. Profitability rises. The mentor's workload becomes more manageable, freeing up time for the mentor to do higher level work.

Mentoring is also an effective way for mentors to further their own professional development. Being a mentor requires lawyers to stay up to date on developments in the law and to think more clearly about what they do and why. Mentors learn a great deal in the process of teaching and explaining these things to associates — and by honing their communication and management skills, which in turn helps them deal more effectively with colleagues, clients, juries, and people in the office. In addition, mentoring a protégé whose talents complement the mentor's own can enlarge and strengthen the mentor's capabilities. For instance, a mentor who is a strategist and favors the big picture might choose to mentor someone who prefers to focus on details. This broadens the mentor's perspective, expands the mentor's abilities, and enables the mentor to serve clients more effectively.

Being a mentor can enhance a lawyer's reputation and leadership and advance the mentor's career. When a protégé excels, others recognize that the mentor can identify and develop talent. Successive mentoring relationships can turn protégés into a supportive power base within the mentor's organization, the legal community, and the business world. Mentors who aspire to or who achieve leadership positions can usually count on their protégés to lend support and follow their lead. Once in positions of leadership, mentors can personally prepare their protégés to succeed them. By introducing protégés to contacts in their professional and business networks, mentors strengthen their own contacts and make new ones. Then protégés who move into positions of influence can become sources of contacts, referrals, and future work for their mentors.

Mentoring helps mentors stay flexible, adaptable, and interested in their work. As lawyers progress in their careers, they may lose sight of the changes going on around them. Hearing a younger person's perspective helps them appreciate and adapt more easily to a rapidly changing world. Being a mentor also can bring renewed excitement, purpose, and meaning to the mentor's work. Mid-career is often a time for reappraisal of the past and planning for the future. Mentors who are bored or tired after many years of doing the same kind of work can convert mid-career ennui into creative energy by helping someone else. If lawyers consider making changes in their own careers, their experience as a mentor makes it easier for them to seek and use mentoring assistance.

Many mentors find pleasure and fulfillment in helping another lawyer succeed. It is satisfying for mentors to know that they play a role in a lawyer's efforts to face the challenges of practice. Mentoring also reaffirms the mentor's own valuable talents and capabilities as a practitioner, teacher, and adviser. Many successful lawyers feel isolated and alone, even within large organizations. Mentoring relationships enable successful lawyers to feel admired by and close to another person.

For some lawyers, mentoring has a higher professional purpose. They may wish to honor their own mentors by continuing the mentoring process to the next generation. Since a mentor's contributions live on in the contributions of protégés, this may be a lawyer's way of leaving a legacy. Still other lawyers act as mentors in order to fulfill what they believe to be an ethical responsibility to promote continued excellence, high standards, and integrity in the profession.

THE IMPORTANCE OF MENTORING FOR WOMEN AND MINORITY LAWYERS

Mentors can have a potent impact on retention and career advancement for women and minority lawyers. These lawyers need mentors who can act as guides and interpreters, and who can help them become part of the social, political, and information networks within their organizations. The Center for Creative Leadership reports that women and minorities are far less likely to have mentors to assist them in making career decisions and that they tend to have less understanding of how to get ahead in their organizations. Studies have found that women and minorities face formidable barriers to advancement because of lack of effective career planning and organizational savvy — exactly the kind of assistance and information that mentors can provide.[1] But mentoring relationships occur less frequently for women and minority lawyers, and in law firms the quality of the mentoring they receive is inconsistent and inequitable according to the NALP Foundation's *Perceptions of Partnership* study. African-American attorneys, for example, consistently report that they have difficulty finding mentors.[2]

In part, this is because people tend to become mentors to those to whom they relate most easily — i.e., people who are like themselves. Since most potential high-level law firm mentors are partners, and most law firm partners are white men, the availability of informal mentors for women and minority lawyers is restricted. Stereotypes, misperceptions, and the complexities of cross-gender and cross-race relationships further impede the natural formation of mentoring relationships for women and minority lawyers.

---

[1] See Ruderman and Ohlott in the References at the conclusion of this book.
[2] See Wilkins.

Mentoring benefits all lawyers but has special importance for lawyers who are outside the mainstream culture of the organization. Because of their outsider status, women and minority lawyers have additional burdens when they enter the workplace. They are perceived and treated differently, and are not privy to the information available through informal workplace networks. The career and psychosocial functions of mentors take on a broader dimension and heightened value for these lawyers. Mentors can bring these lawyers into informal social and professional networks that conquer feelings of alienation and build a sense of connectedness to the firm. Mentors provide access to "inside" information, plum assignments, and influential partners and clients. They inform associates about the politics and unwritten rules of practice and offer guidance about how to present and position themselves in the organization. As sponsors, mentors can broadcast and promote the associate's abilities and contributions, and help build the associate's reputation. Mentors can move past common stereotypes and misperceptions to see the real talents these lawyers bring to the firm.

Let's take a look at some of the barriers that make mentoring so critical — and so elusive — for women and minority lawyers.

■ BARRIERS FOR WOMEN

With few exceptions, women lawyers are outside the mainstream law firm culture which is defined by and for men. The rules of this culture are foreign to women, and those who succeed have to adapt not just to the world of law practice generally but also to a culture where institutional definitions of success may conflict with their own.[1] Many women do so at greater personal sacrifice than is required of male lawyers. Studies have documented, for example, that women lawyers are less likely to marry or have children and more likely to divorce than their male colleagues.[2]

Research confirms that mentoring is a critical success factor for women but that, for most women, mentoring does not happen naturally.

---

[1] M. N. Ruderman, P. J. Ohlott, K. Panzer, and S. N. King, "How Managers View Success: Perspectives of High Achieving Women," *Leadership in Action*, Center for Creative Leadership and Jossey-Bass Publishers, Vol. 18, No. 6, 1999.

[2] Patrick J. Schiltz, "On Being Happy, Healthy, and Ethical," *Vanderbilt Law Review*, May 1999.

A 1996 Catalyst survey of executive women found that 37 percent cited "having an influential mentor" as a critical factor in their career success. Research also shows, however, that women have difficulty finding mentors and that the lack of mentors is an impediment to their advancement. In a 1999 Catalyst study of 1,735 executive women of color in corporate management, 47 percent cited lack of an influential mentor or sponsor as a barrier to advancement. These women were already in management and more than half of them held graduate degrees, yet they were unable to find influential mentors who could help them move into higher positions of leadership in their companies. The NALP Foundation's *Perceptions of Partnership* study confirms these findings in the legal profession.

The reasons why women have a harder time finding mentors are numerous and complex. One of the major issues is the limited number of potential women mentors. Women now make up about half of all law school graduates, slightly over 40 percent of law firm associates, 37 percent of in-house counsel, and 29 percent of all lawyers. But 1999 data show that only 14.6 percent of law firm partners are women and only 44 general counsel of Fortune 500 companies are women.[1] This limits the number of high-level women mentors and role models for women associates. A further constraint is that women who are partners are not necessarily available or desirable to young women as mentors. Because of the greater family demands on women, many women partners have no time to be mentors — and many women associates do not have time to look for mentors. Some senior women feel no obligation to mentor younger women lawyers. As one woman partner explained, "I've spent my whole career in this firm telling them to treat me as a lawyer, not a woman. I've succeeded without a mentor, and so can they."

For their part, young women lawyers are not always drawn to women partners as potential mentors. For many of these young women, the experiences of older women and the compromises they made seem irrelevant. In their eyes, these senior women succeeded under circumstances significantly different from those facing women who are starting legal careers today. A lot of young women also perceive women partners as less powerful or influential than their male counterparts and therefore less able to help advance their careers. Consequently, they

---

[1] Jane Pigott and Stephen E. Nowlan, "Success Strategies from Women at the Top," *Diversity & The Bar*, Minority Corporate Counsel Association, August 1999.

believe that men in the firm will offer them better opportunities, sounder career advice, and more political protection.

But, for many reasons, men do not readily mentor women. Many men assume that women are not fully committed to their careers and will leave the profession to care for husbands and children. Male partners and male corporate counsel do not share the same natural affinity, commonalities, and comfort level with women attorneys that they share with other men. They worry about how to deal with women lawyers during business travel and in social settings. Many of these men are wary of giving women the type of close individual attention that mentoring involves. They are put off by the complexities of the relationships between men and women in a workplace where the rules are changing and the risks of sexual involvement and perceived harassment are grave. Rather than deal with such quandaries, these men avoid them by refusing to mentor women altogether.

Women also hold views that make them less likely to seek out mentors, male or female. Many women shy away from issues of power and politics. They believe that hard work and merit are the primary determinants of advancement, so they do not pay enough attention to forging ties with influential power brokers who might serve as mentors. They do not appreciate the commanding role of politics in the organizations where they work, so they do not engage in the kind of networking and mentoring relationships necessary to get ahead. Even women who do recognize the importance of networking and finding influential mentors often have family commitments that limit the time they have available to engage in these activities.

■ BARRIERS FOR MINORITY ATTORNEYS

The importance of mentoring for minority attorneys is also well established.[1] In *Breaking Through: The Making of Minority Executives in Corporate America*, authors David A. Thomas and John J. Gabarro note that one of the things that distinguishes minority executives who have reached the top of the corporate ladder from their white counterparts is that they built twice as many relationships with mentors during their early careers. Likewise, in a 1998 study conducted by

---

[1] See *Perceptions of Partnership* and Wilkins in the References at the conclusion of this book.

Columbia University and Korn/Ferry of 280 minority professionals with salaries of $100,000 to $500,000, more than half of the minority executives said that formal and informal mentoring played a key role in their careers.

Minority attorneys now constitute nearly 20 percent of law school graduates, 11.8 percent of law firm associates, and 9 percent of in-house counsel. These minority attorneys have a hard time finding mentors like themselves because the number of minority partners and senior corporate attorneys is so small. In 1998, only 3.07 percent of the more than 40,000 law firm partners nationwide were minority lawyers. In a survey of Fortune 1000 companies conducted in late 1998, in the 301 companies that responded, ethnic minority lawyers represented only 4.3 percent of the general counsel and 8.6 percent of attorneys who report directly to the general counsel. Minority attorneys clearly have difficulties finding high-level mentors who are likely role models and who share similar backgrounds and experiences.

Although firms heavily recruit minority candidates, they do little after these lawyers arrive to make them feel a part of the firm or to overcome their sense of being an outsider. Mentoring can help minority attorneys overcome their isolation, but informal mentoring relationships rarely develop. Minority attorneys frequently remain excluded from the social and personal networks of majority partners, both inside and outside of the office. White male partners who feel more comfortable and at ease with other white men overlook minority attorneys in client development efforts and do not invite minority attorneys to social and cultural events they attend with white colleagues. Since many of the personal relationships among lawyers in a firm develop during these "out of office" events, minority lawyers lose the opportunity to form such personal relationships.

In terms of legal work, minority attorneys are often reluctant to seek advice from partners for fear that it will fuel the misperception that they are not qualified or cannot make it as a lawyer. At the same time, potential mentors shy away from minority lawyers because they believe that establishing a relationship with an attorney of color will be too complicated and require too much effort. Many minority attorneys have to overcome negative stereotypes and a "presumption of incompetence." Because their ability is in doubt, they receive less challenging work assignments and are subjected to a higher degree of scrutiny. Potential mentors perceive a greater risk in mentoring a minority attorney whose performance will be more closely watched and whose failure may be attributed to the mentor. Without mentors to advise them about assignments, career moves, and office politics, or to promote their interests, minority lawyers often feel they are treated unfairly and miss career advancement opportunities.

Minority lawyers also need mentors who can provide periodic reality checks. With few other attorneys like them in the firm, they may exaggerate minor fears, doubts, and worries. When minority lawyers feel like outsiders, they do not know whether their perceptions reflect reality. As Doug, a young Asian-American associate, put it, "Am I being hypersensitive to consider it racist when a partner keeps talking about a 'Chinese wall' instead of an 'ethical wall'?" These types of concerns occur daily for minority lawyers, and having a mentor to discuss them with will prevent the concerns from growing and festering.

Minority professionals spend more time than their majority counterparts working through issues regarding their professional identity and feelings of alienation and exclusion. It is especially important for minority professionals to have a network of mentors that includes one or more mentors from their minority group. Mentors who are not in the same minority group can also be effective, provided they understand the unique concerns and frustrations minority attorneys experience related to race or ethnicity. These may include:

- Their differences being perceived as deficits;

- The beliefs of others that they are less competent;

- Having to work harder to overcome others' doubts about their ability;

- Being held to a higher standard;

- Self-doubt ("If others think I am not good enough, maybe I'm not");

- Less "forgiveness" for their mistakes;

- Having failures attributed to their minority group;

- Having their successes deemed "exceptional";

- Being subjected to subtle daily insults (e.g., the court bailiff assumes a black attorney is a defendant);

- Social isolation;

- Lack of role models and peers with whom they identify; and

- Tokenism (e.g., being invited to a client meeting to display the firm's diversity, but then not being assigned to the client's work).[1]

By being aware of and sensitive to these issues, mentors can help minority attorneys get past the obstacles that interfere with their professional aspirations.

---

[1] Ida Abbott, "Mentoring Plays a Key Role in Retaining Attorneys of Color," *Law Governance Review*, Spring 1998.

CHAPTER 4

MENTORING PROBLEMS AND HOW TO OVERCOME THEM

"With relationships, we give up
predictability for potentials"

MARGARET J. WHEATLEY

Mentoring is undeniably valuable and important, but that does not mean it is risk-free. As with any relationship based on trust, there are personal threats; as with any relationship centered on work, there are political and professional perils to watch out for. Risks cannot be eliminated but they can be minimized with careful planning, heightened awareness, and a realistic set of expectations. Here are some of the most common problems.

■ UNSUCCESSFUL RELATIONSHIPS

People usually enter a mentoring relationship with anticipation and high hopes for a good experience, but not all mentoring relationships work out well. Sometimes the mentor turns out to be less able, thoughtful, or effective than promised at the start. Janice, a fourth-year litigation associate, entered her mentoring relationship with great excitement. Her mentor was a woman litigation partner whom the associates in the firm viewed as a wonderful role model. But the mentor turned out to be curt, manipulative, and unresponsive to Janice's concerns. Instead of listening to Janice, she told Janice what to do and how to do it. She frequently canceled meetings and she accepted phone calls and interruptions during the few mentoring sessions they had. Janice felt that the mentor never really got to know her and took no real interest in the issues Janice needed to deal with. Janice's high hopes were never realized.

Mentors, too, can be disappointed. One partner expressed her frustration and disappointment over David, an associate who left the firm after more than a year into their excellent mentoring relationship. David had assured her that he loved the firm and was looking forward to becoming a partner. When he decided to move to another city to be closer to his family, the mentor was crushed. "I invested so much of my time in David. I don't know if I can do it again — or if I should bother with anyone else. I'm mentally and emotionally exhausted." The fact that David gave his mentor superior marks in his exit interview did little to mitigate her letdown.

■ BREACH OF TRUST

Mentoring relationships are focused on helping another person. Mentors and associates invest their trust as well as their time in each other. To make a mentoring relationship work effectively, the mentor and protégé must be able to share information and knowledge they would withhold in less intense relationships. When either mentor or protége is self-serving or self-centered, the relationship is damaged and the mentoring partner is personally harmed. That is what happened to Jim, a law firm administrator. For two years, Jim acted as a mentor to his assistant, Andrew. Jim taught Andrew everything he needed to know about the job and the firm. Jim advised Andrew, promoted him, and touted his abilities to the firm's management team. Jim also confided in Andrew that he lacked certain technology skills and had enrolled in some courses to learn them. Andrew betrayed this confidence during discussions with the Executive Director when he told her that Jim was unable to handle the department's work adequately because his knowledge of technology was out of date. Andrew deliberately failed to mention Jim's imminent plan to learn those skills but did mention that he personally had considerable expertise in the area. The Executive Director wisely asked Jim about the situation and was satisfied with Jim's plan to acquire further training. Andrew's betrayal of Jim soured their relationship and effectively cut Andrew's own career at the firm short. Nonetheless, Jim felt personally hurt and betrayed.

Not all betrayals within a mentoring relationship are as malicious as Andrew's. But people who are insensitive and self-aggrandizing, or who promote their own interests at the expense of their mentoring partner, will cause the relationship to break down.

■ OVER-RELIANCE

One important purpose of mentoring is to help young lawyers become more independent and more secure in their own abilities. So when mentors counsel protégés, they have to be careful or protégés may fall into the trap of over-relying on their mentor's advice. If mentors provide answers or solutions, they may shift the responsibility for making a decision away from the protégé, where the responsibility belongs. If the protégé accepts the mentor's advice uncritically, learning and growth are curtailed.

Mentors are supposed to help protégés solve problems, but they should not solve the problems for their protégés. Mentors may be tempted to rescue protégés from difficult situations and to cover their mistakes. When mentors do jump in with solutions, associates do not learn how to handle their own mistakes and problems, and their development is stifled. If this happens repeatedly, the protégé becomes dependent, which contradicts the very purpose of the mentoring relationship.

■ BAD ADVICE

Mentors are not always wise, especially when offering advice about someone else's career. They may be well meaning, but the effects on the protégé may be quite damaging. Mentors may misunderstand or misjudge a situation, try to help in an area where they are not qualified, or assume that what works well for them will also work for the protégé.

Jane, for example, was a happy second-year trust and estates lawyer whose mentor was a powerful litigation partner in the same firm. Although Jane had no interest at all in litigation, her mentor advised her to get some trial experience to make herself more valuable to the firm. Believing that her mentor knew best what she needed for advancement, Jane spent a miserable year handling a nasty lawsuit and a three-week trial. The case consumed most of her time and diverted her from developing additional expertise in the field she loved, trusts and estates. At the end of the year, Jane was depressed and much of the trust work that would normally have gone to her was being given to other lawyers. Because the mentor's advice reflected his own interests, not Jane's, it had unfortunate consequences for Jane's life and career.

■ AN OVERLY CONTROLLING MENTOR

Occasionally, mentors abuse the powerful influence they have over protégés. Mentors may try to replicate themselves or to make the protégé dependent on them. Rather than try to help the associate develop a personal style, these mentors insist that their way is the only way. They do not see themselves as one role model among many; they demand that the associate follow their lead exactly. These individuals are dangerous to an associate's career. By trying to control everything the associate does, this type of mentor can be suffocating. If the associate refuses to follow the mentor's directions, these mentors can become vindictive.

Most mentors are not as controlling, and the few who are tend to be far more subtle. Take the case of Mark and Susan. Mark, a young partner who specialized in health care law, moved to another firm to start the firm's health law department. He invited Susan, a promising young associate, to go with him, and Susan accepted. Over the years, Mark's prominence and power grew. He brought in work and Susan did the work. In fact, he kept Susan so busy on his clients' work that she had no clients of her own. Mark successfully sponsored Susan for partnership. Even after Susan was a partner, however, Mark discouraged her from seeking her own clients, grew angry whenever Susan tried to become more independent, and criticized her for being distracted from the important work she had to do for him. As a consequence, Susan never rose above the first tier in the partnership and was unable to move to another law firm because she had no clients of her own. She was trapped. In the guise of being her mentor, Mark took Susan under his wing so tightly that she was not able to break free.

■ A MISMATCH WITH THE "WRONG" MENTOR

Not all mentors are the right mentor for an individual. There are many reasons that a mentor who is otherwise perfectly competent may not be suitable for a particular protégé. A "wrong" mentor may simply be one whose abilities are not suited to the protégé's needs. An associate who wants to learn about trial skills will not learn those skills from a corporate lawyer. Similarly, if an ambitious protégé wants to rub elbows with the company's executives, a mentor without political clout or savvy will not serve the protégé's needs.

Sometimes even a good mentor can turn out to be "wrong" when circumstances change. Howard was Ann's mentor and he was great to her. They worked together on many matters and Howard's partners identified Ann with him and his practice. Unfortunately, Howard left to join a competitor firm which did not have room for any associates, so Ann stayed behind. The firm was angry about Howard's defection and took it out on Ann. Even though Ann's work was good and she was well-liked, she got caught in the political cross-fire caused by her mentor.

■ DOUBLE DEPARTURES

One of the risks of mentoring for law firms is that lawyers who work closely together in mentoring relationships may leave together to go elsewhere. Unlike the situation of Howard and Ann, many partners who leave law firms take talented associates with them, especially if they have trained and mentored those associates. Strong mentors who decide to move to another firm, or who break off to start their own firm, have little difficulty attracting their current and former protégés to join them. This turns into a double whammy for the law firm.

■ MENTOR JEALOUSY

In a mentoring relationship, the mentor helps a less experienced lawyer gain the experience, knowledge, and support to move ahead in the firm and in the profession. Over time, the mentored lawyer acquires enough competence and polish to become the mentor's peer, and, ultimately, the protégé may surpass the mentor in terms of professional expertise, reputation, influence, or accomplishment.

Most mentors are justifiably proud when the lawyers they mentor move ahead, but some mentors may become jealous. In extreme cases, mentors who envy the accomplishments of their protégés have been known to sabotage them. Sara had a mentor who was always ready to help her. He was happy that Sara shared his interest in a specialized area of tax law and spent a great deal of time teaching Sara the fine points of that practice. They had what Sara felt was a very positive mentoring relationship until Sara became recognized as an expert in the field. When Sara received invitations to speak at conferences instead of her mentor, his attitude changed. Instead of being supportive, he became critical of Sara and even tried to undermine her reputation by disparaging her abilities to colleagues. When Sara learned what he was doing, their relationship ended with hurt feelings on both sides.

■ TOO FEW ROLE MODELS

Lawyers need more than one role model in order to discern what they feel comfortable with — what works for them and what does not. Having only one mentor can be a problem for impressionable young lawyers. Working closely with a mentor narrows the protégés' field of vision. They do not see the range of behaviors, styles, skills, and attitudes that can produce career success. Protégés may fail to distinguish good practices from bad ones, or they may adopt behaviors and styles that are effective for the mentor but totally inappropriate for them. This is a common risk for protégés who work with charismatic mentors. These protégés may be influenced so strongly that they copy the mentor's identity instead of finding their own.

For law firm associates, it is also important for political reasons to have exposure to many partners in the firm. When partnership decisions are made, an associate who is seen as tied to a particular partner, or who has not worked with a number of different partners, may not have broad enough support to be elected a partner. Other partners may not know the associate well enough to judge whether he or she is partnership material.

■ INTIMACY AND ROMANCE

See Chapter Six for comments on the challenges intimacy and romance can pose within a mentoring relationship.

Dealing with Mentoring Problems

Any human relationship carries risks as well as benefits, and mentoring relationships are no exception. Mentors and protégés can be selfish, manipulative, and foolish, causing adverse consequences to the other person and the relationship. The modern approach to mentoring provides some protection to mentors and protégés who find themselves in difficult mentoring relationships. It is important, though, for lawyers to be resilient. One bad mentoring relationship should not deter a lawyer from moving on to others that may prove to be more satisfying and worthwhile.

Some of the measures lawyers can take to protect themselves from problematic mentoring relationships are described below. These measures cannot guarantee that mentoring relationships will be problem-free, but they increase the likelihood of a good mentoring experience.

- Limit expectations and agree on mentoring goals together at the beginning of the relationship.

- Build trust, maintain open communication, and pay close attention to each other. Be alert for warning signs.

- Keep mentoring goals in mind. When these goals are clear, the parties are better able to recognize signals that the mentoring relationship is off track.

- Reduce reliance on any one person for career assistance by engaging in more than one mentoring relationship.

- Have a network of mentors. A network affords a variety of role models.

- Seek work assignments that expose the protégé to many different potential mentors and role models.

- Remember that each lawyer is ultimately responsible for his or her own career choices. A mentor's advice should be carefully weighed, but decisions should be based on independent judgment.

- Protégés who have doubts or worries about their mentors should seek guidance from someone else. In a formal mentoring program, that person is usually the program coordinator. For political reasons, it may be best to go to someone outside the protégé's firm or department such as a friend, family member, or other professional colleague.

■ Protégés should assume much of the responsibility for the mentoring relationship. When protégés take responsibility, they have "permission" to leave relationships that are unsatisfactory.

■ Request a new mentor if you are a protégé in a formal mentoring program and the current relationship is unsatisfactory.

■ Allow mentoring relationships to continue. Mentoring relationships do not need to end when a mentor or protégé leaves the firm. The specific nature of the relationship may change, but it can continue even when the mentor and protégé no longer work together.

■ Learn from bad mentoring experiences. Albeit difficult, they may be a valuable way to learn how to cope with and surmount challenging situations. Use this knowledge to make your next mentoring relationship more successful.

CHAPTER 5

How to Start, Maintain, and Conclude Mentoring Relationships

"A sense of belonging is something humans need if they are to commit themselves to more than simple selfishness."

CHARLES HANDY

Starting a Mentoring Relationship

■ Becoming a Mentor

Prospective mentors need to find someone who will make their investment of time and attention worthwhile. If you want to be a mentor, look for someone who seems to be promising, whose professional interests are amenable to your own, and who has a compatible attitude, work ethic, and personality. Before approaching a potential protégé, consider what you have to offer. As a prospective mentor, you have many talents, skills, and abilities that can be of great benefit to someone else. What are your strengths? How can you help a protégé? What are you willing to give? Think back to the best mentors you have had and the various ways they helped you. What was it about those individuals that makes you think about them as mentors? What did they do? What qualities did they exhibit? What did you learn? How did the mentor help you learn? How did you benefit from those mentoring relationships? Exploring these questions will help you determine the ways that you can best assist someone else along their career journey.

Lawyers about to embark on a mentoring relationship should also give some thought to what they will expect in return for their mentoring assistance. If you want something more than the satisfaction of helping a fellow lawyer grow professionally (e.g., employer recognition), make sure that your potential protégé understands and agrees.

A key to starting a productive relationship is finding a good match. In addition to mutual admiration, your abilities and the protégé's needs must complement each other. In particular, the help you proffer must be needed, appropriate, and timely for the protégé. For various reasons, a prospective mentor may be drawn to a potential protégé who may not need or want what the mentor can provide. You cannot assume that all lawyers will be receptive to you as a mentor. For practical or personal reasons, a relationship may not be possible. There may be scheduling conflicts, the potential protégé may not have the right frame of mind to engage in a mentoring relationship, or the lawyer may not have time in his or her life for a mentoring relationship.

■ FINDING A MENTOR

Lawyers often complain that they cannot find mentors. There are mentors to be found, but the search must be undertaken purposefully and strategically. To begin, you have to be clear about three things: what you want from a mentoring relationship, what you can contribute to a mentoring relationship, and why someone should want to be your mentor.

First, decide what you hope to gain from a mentoring relationship. Without this understanding, you cannot identify the people who might be able to help you. Do you want to improve your ability to manage competing work demands? Do you wish to become well known as a conference speaker? The former requires a mentor who is well organized and can show you some practical techniques and strategies; the latter needs a mentor with contacts, influence, and perhaps good presentation skills. A potential mentor may be perfect for one purpose but not for another.

Also consider what you can offer a potential mentor. Mentoring relationships are reciprocal; it is not enough to focus on your self-interest alone. You will have to contribute to the mentoring relationship in some meaningful way. It may be a technical skill, important contacts, or simply your eagerness to learn, which is sufficient motivation for many people to serve as mentors. Occasionally mentors will have specific expectations for protégés. Some mentors may want you to put in extra hours over and above the time you already spend at work. Still other mentors may expect you to become a disciple. Think about what you can offer and what you are willing to do in order to make a mentoring relationship work.

You also have to be clear about why you believe that someone should agree to be your mentor. Be honest with yourself; this is no time for modesty. You must believe in your own potential in order to persuade someone that being your mentor is worth their time and effort. Assess your needs, your talents, and your ambitions. The clearer you are about what you hope to gain from a mentoring relationship, the easier it will be to articulate why a potential mentor should help you achieve your goals.

Once you are clear about your desired goals, your possible contributions, and your worthiness as a protégé, you can start your search for a suitable mentor. The initial step is to identify some potential mentors. Networking is an invaluable way to do this. For many people networking suggests manipulating others for personal gain, but that is certainly not what is meant here. Contrary to its negative connotation, networking is an important ingredient for career advancement. Across organizations, it is an efficient way to locate needed resources, learn about job opportunities, and market your reputation and services. Within organizations, having a strong network of people to draw upon for assistance can be a major factor contributing to career success.[1] Networking is an excellent and important way to meet potential mentors.

What exactly is networking? It is the process of conscientiously building and maintaining a web of personal relationships through the mutual exchange of information, advice, resources, referrals, and support. It involves staying alert for opportunities to meet and get to know people who might be able to help you and whom you can help in return. People who network effectively are generous with their own

---

[1] See Kelley and Hill in the References at the conclusion of this book.

time and abilities. They go out of their way to help others and to establish strong personal relationships. Consequently, when they ask for help, people are usually glad to oblige.

Your personal network may already include several potential mentors or you may need to go out and find some new ones. Where should you look? Potential mentors can be located wherever you can find people who match the description of the mentor you are seeking. This includes your workplace, business and professional organizations, community groups of all kinds, or personal interest groups. (Chapter Eleven discusses several types of organizations where lawyers can meet potential mentors.)

Usually, the best place to begin looking for mentors is in your own workplace. If your firm has a mentoring program, take advantage of it. Don't worry if the mentor assigned to you does not suit all of your needs. He or she is only one member of your mentoring "board of advisors." If your firm does not have a mentoring program, identify a pool of potential mentors in the office. Lawyers who practice alone or in very small firms generally have to look outside the office for potential mentors. (See Chapter Eleven.)

Many lawyers find it advisable to have at least one mentor who does not work in the same office. These mentors can be especially valuable resources for problems that deal with professional and personal insecurities. When a problem involves emotional or personal dilemmas, such as work/family concerns, persons outside the firm may be more objective and forthcoming in their advice. Even if there are people in your firm whom you trust regarding such confidential matters, outside mentors can often offer broader perspectives, suggestions, and reality checks without the risk of repercussions within the organization.

Do not limit yourself to mentors who are lawyers; non-lawyers can teach you important practice skills. Business people and mediators can help you become a better negotiator; accountants can show you how to analyze complex financial data; insurance and advertising executives can offer insights into marketing and selling professional services. What you learn is easily transferable to legal practice. In return, you can offer mentors in other fields your professional skills, perspectives, and contacts.

After you identify a pool of potential mentors, you still need to select and get to know an individual who would be a suitable mentor for you by observing and researching possible candidates. Look for someone whose style and practice you admire, who seems to share an interest of yours, and who has the talents, knowledge, clients, or contacts that might be able to help you. In particular, consider how that person can help you achieve your goals and be sure that the individual's abilities match your needs. Determine who might have the time, patience, and inclination to become your mentor; whom you would enjoy working with; who might be willing to be your mentor; and what might motivate them to do so. Find out as much as possible about the potential mentor, including whether the person has been a mentor before, how the person performed as a mentor, whether he or she has the particular skills and attributes you are looking for, and whether the potential mentor is under any special pressures that may prevent him or her from taking on a mentoring responsibility. Seek out information about the potential mentor's professional values, goals, and ambitions, and whether they are compatible with yours.

A potential mentor may not be apparent at first. Sharon, for example, was a junior associate assigned to work with Sam, a powerful but disagreeable litigation partner. Sam was abrupt, rude, and extremely demanding, and most associates hated working with him. Rather than view Sam negatively, Sharon welcomed Sam's directness and high expectations. When he was rude to her, she called him on it — and he apologized. Because Sharon's work and dedication met his high expectations, Sam began to direct more challenging assignments to her. Their styles and personalities were dramatically different, but the two grew to respect each other and Sam gradually became a mentor to Sharon.

One of the reasons Sharon and Sam respected each other was that they both placed the highest value on superior legal work and strict ethical standards. Sharing common professional values is vital to the success of a mentoring relationship. Mentor and protégé may not hold all of the same values, but there must be sufficient commonality for the two to trust and respect each other. These feelings are not necessary for learning to take place, since you can learn by observing any individual with the skills or behaviors that interest you. But you cannot sustain a mentoring relationship with someone you dislike, disrespect, or distrust.

When you identify the prospective mentor, you will need a strategy for approaching him or her. If you know the potential mentor, you can be either direct or indirect. If you feel comfortable doing so, ask directly for the help you need. Otherwise, start indirectly by asking to work with the person on a particular matter, offering to work on a pet project, volunteering to help with some administrative chore, or joining the person on the firm's softball team. The important point is to create a situation where you interact with this person frequently. During those interactions, work hard, be effective and enthusiastic, and make yourself someone the potential mentor thinks well of.

If it is an individual you do not know personally, try to find someone who will introduce or refer you, or look for opportunities to meet the prospective mentor. Again, this is where your networking efforts will reward you. Arrange to meet the person privately, explore areas of common interest, and get a sense of whether he or she would be a good — and willing — mentor for you. Even if you feel optimistic, it is unlikely that someone will agree to be your mentor after only one meeting. Follow up, establish a good rapport, and stay in touch with this person. Once a relationship is established and you believe this person would be a good mentor for you, you can request his or her mentoring assistance. No matter how you establish the relationship, when the time seems right, move to the next step, asking for mentoring help.

When asking someone to be your mentor, be as prepared and specific as possible. If you have done your homework in identifying the prospective mentor, you will be able to explain why that person has the skills and capabilities to help you, how they will benefit, and why they should be your mentor. Some potential mentors may balk at the notion of mentoring because they think of mentoring as a long-term, comprehensive, and burdensome commitment. In approaching a potential mentor, you do not need to use the term "mentoring" at all. Instead, be precise about what you would like the mentor to do and why. Describe your goals, be clear about what you want, and estimate the time it will take. Be ready to respond to any concerns the potential mentor may raise about the nature, duration, or scope of the commitment you are requesting. Be realistic about the substance of the request. Be tactful and professional in your approach.

Many lawyers worry that asking for help will make them appear weak or insecure, which will turn off a potential mentor. The key is to present your request in a manner that is thoughtful, mature, and self-assured. Emphasize your own responsibilities in the mentoring partnership. If you feel confident about your abilities and are clear about what you want and how this mentor will help you become a better lawyer, your request for mentoring assistance will make you seem astute, not needy. If you are anxious, it may be helpful to practice what you will say with a friend before the meeting takes place.

Do not expect or insist on an immediate response. The potential mentor may need time to think about your proposal. If so, arrange for a follow-up meeting. If the potential mentor declines, do not take it personally. Tactfully try to find out why the person said no and whether he or she would be receptive to a mentoring proposal at another time or with a more limited scope. Even if a potential mentor declines your offer, he or she will be flattered that you asked for his or her advice. Occasionally, candidates who decline an invitation will offer to refer you to other potential mentors. In any case, thank the person for their consideration and for being direct and honest with you.

Maintaining Mentoring Relationships: Key Mentoring Practices

Certain mentoring practices enable mentors and protégés to derive the maximum benefit from a mentoring experience. Linda Phillips-Jones, Ph.D., developed a "mentoring skills model" based on certain competencies needed by mentors and protégés. The figure below is a variation of that model, adapted for lawyers and identifying key mentoring practices. Employing these practices will yield the optimum benefit for the mentoring parties. Most of these are common practices among lawyers, and all can be learned and strengthened during the mentoring process. Legal employers can facilitate the development of these practices by providing training in mentoring skills. Such training is an essential element of formal mentoring programs (see Chapter Six), but can be provided independently to promote and enhance informal workplace mentoring as well.

Diagram 1.
Key Mentoring Practices

■ KEY PRACTICES OF BOTH MENTORS AND PROTÉGÉS

Empathy. Empathy goes to the heart of an effective mentoring relationship. Daniel Goleman, author of two leading books on emotional intelligence, describes empathy as "our social radar" because it is how we sense what others feel without their saying so. Empathy enables individuals to be more sensitive and responsive to the unspoken needs, feelings, and idiosyncrasies that others bring to mentoring relationships. All of us bring our own attitudes, beliefs, and life experiences to our interactions with others. We also bring our fears, insecurities, and neuroses. All of those factors create a filter through which we judge the people we meet, and most people assume that other people see things the same way. Empathy reminds us that other people see the world differently and enables us to adapt to others in the course of our interactions.

Below are some examples of situations where lawyers' perceptions and feelings interfered with the mentoring process. In each case, someone with empathy salvaged a relationship which otherwise would have failed.

■ Martha, an attorney with seven years of legal experience, joined the legal department of a large health care company. When she arrived at her new office, she was greeted by her assigned mentor, who had been a lawyer for only two years. The mentor tried to be helpful by dropping into Martha's office every day to explain office politics and ask if she had any questions he could answer. Never having had a mentor before, Martha felt suspicious. She felt she was being watched and resented having someone with less legal experience giving her advice. Sensing that something was bothering her about their relationship, the mentor invited her to lunch and elicited Martha's feelings. By explaining that the purpose of the mentoring program was simply to put new lawyers at ease and by offering to leave her alone if she preferred, the mentor was able to assuage Martha's concerns and overcome her misunderstanding and mistrust.

■ Alec was being mentored informally by Mitch, a junior partner in his department. Although Alec enjoyed working with Mitch, he soon realized that Mitch was behaving oddly. He snapped at people, disappeared from his office for hours at a time without explanation, and looked tired all the time. Alec asked other lawyers about Mitch's behavior and was assured that Mitch was "under the same stress we're all feeling." One afternoon after Mitch got angry over something trivial, Alec asked Mitch if he was all right. He told Mitch of his observations and expressed his concern. Mitch broke down, explaining that his son was in serious trouble at school and that this was causing strain on the whole family. Mitch had not realized how his stress was affecting his behavior in the office and his relationship with Alec. As they talked, Alec was able to console Mitch and persuade him to seek professional help.

■ Joyce was an African-American associate. Her assigned mentor, a litigation partner, was also the writing instructor in the firm's legal writing course for associates. Although she liked her mentor personally, Joyce believed that she was given this particular mentor because the firm assumed that, as an African-American woman, she would need help with her legal writing skills. The mentor, noting that Joyce avoided meeting with him, reached out to her to find out what was wrong. He sensed her discomfort but did not know the source — and told her so. He was able to open a dialogue that unearthed her feelings and enabled him to reassure her that their match had nothing to do with her race or his role in the writing program.

Effective communication. It is essential for a mentor and protégé to communicate clearly, openly, and regularly. Good communication is more than simply speaking to each other. It requires attentive listening and meaningful discourse. It means trying to see the world through the other person's eyes without making judgments and expressing one's thoughts freely and coherently in a search for common understanding. This is not easy to do when lawyers are under pressure with many competing demands on their time and attention. Yet, when they get together to discuss the protégé's development or concerns, it is essential that mentor and protégé be fully engaged in dialogue. For serious conversations, set aside time to meet. If it is impossible to find a place in the office that is free from interruptions, go out for a walk or a cappuccino. Mentoring does not have to take place in the office and in fact, communication may be freer and easier in a more relaxed setting.

Listening is a critical mentoring practice. Attentive listening tells a speaker that we genuinely care about what he or she says, which is fundamental to the formation of trust. Careful listening is necessary for a mentor to get a true understanding of what the protégé thinks, wants, and needs. Mentors have to listen not just to the protégé's words but to the assumptions and beliefs behind the words in order to reach the deeper meaning of a protégé's questions and statements. Mentors need to stay alert both for comments of obvious significance and for clues that may be more subtle — and then to act on what they hear. By following up with questions that challenge the protégé's assumptions or seek clarification, mentors can help protégés develop more profound understanding and growth.

Mentors must also be careful in conveying information to the protégé. Because they have their protégé's trust, mentors have a great deal of influence on the protégé's performance, attitude, and behavior. Their praise and criticism will carry great weight. Mentors must therefore be tactful, but clear and direct, in their communications with protégés. Mentors should encourage their protégés to speak openly and freely, to ask questions when they are unsure, and to challenge the mentor when they disagree. When giving advice or feedback, mentors must be sincere and constructive, offering specific suggestions for making improvements or corrections.

Listening is also a critical part of a protégé's learning experience. Protégés need to listen carefully in order to understand the information, advice, and feedback they receive from the mentor. By listening attentively, protégés demonstrate that they are interested, engaged, and really hearing what the mentor is telling them.

Sharing information, questioning each other, respecting differences of opinion, and seeking mutual understanding are integral to the mentoring process. Mentors and protégés must be honest with each other, or they will lose credibility and trust. Directly acknowledging the other's concerns and feelings is important. If difficulties arise between mentor and protégé, they should try to deal with them promptly and openly.

Commitment. Mentoring requires a commitment of time, attention, and effort. Mentors and protégés should not assume commitments they cannot fulfill, and each should be mindful of the other's time and work constraints. They must be accessible to each other and set aside time for their relationship. If work or personal demands interfere with regular meetings, they should stay in touch by telephone. They should inform each other when, where, and how they can be reached by voice mail, email, and other electronic media and be as flexible as possible to make themselves available.

Mentor and protégé should actively look for opportunities to fulfill mentoring objectives and hold themselves accountable for working toward those objectives. Promises must be kept. Follow-through is essential when offers are extended or projects are undertaken because each individual must be able to count on the other. Protégés should not be discouraged when a busy mentor is hard to reach. When mentors have agreed to meet or speak with their protégés, protégés are entitled and expected to keep trying. If a mentor finds it impossible to adhere to the original mentoring commitment, the mentor should withdraw from the relationship, restrict the scope of responsibilities, or suspend the relationship temporarily to resume it at a later time.

Trustworthiness. A mentoring relationship cannot succeed without mutual trust. Trust takes time to develop and is built in many small steps. For trust to take hold, mentor and protégé must behave in ways that engender trust. They must be able to view each other as professionally competent and worthy mentoring partners, and, although mentor and protégé may never become personal friends, they must earn each other's respect as professionals. Trust deepens over the course of the relationship if mentor and protégé act in ways that are ethical, reliable, credible, open, honest, and consistent, and if they are willing to admit their mistakes, stand behind their word, and give each other appropriate credit and recognition.

■ KEY PRACTICES OF MENTORS

Facilitating learning. Mentoring is less about transmitting information than it is about helping protégés learn how to help themselves. Mentors can suggest and guide, but protégés are in charge of their own learning. One of a mentor's most important functions is to help protégés learn how to practice law. Although mentors do not necessarily teach in a formal sense, they do facilitate learning through work assignments, coaching, and counseling.

Learning to be a lawyer is much more than memorizing legal principles, studying trial skills, or knowing the rules of professional conduct. It requires the development of sound legal judgment through the prudent application of such knowledge. And that kind of learning occurs through experience. Protégés learn what lawyering is all about by observing it in action, processing what they observe with the mentor's help, and applying what they learn to a host of different circumstances. Mentors work with protégés in a context where new knowledge and skills are put to use on real problems. Protégés construct the meaning of this new learning for themselves, but within the context of a relationship with a mentor who can offer guidance and support. That support allows protégés to try out new ideas, styles, and skills with minimal risk.

Mentoring encourages protégés to step back for a moment to reflect on an encounter, conversation, newly learned skill, or experience, and to consider the lessons to be learned from them. Mentors help protégés examine how they think, i.e., how they approach problems, apply their knowledge, and find solutions. Mentors help their protégés see not only the particular assignment or experience before them but the patterns that emerge and the broader context that gives those experiences meaning. Some experiences may be dismal failures while others are wildly successful. Young lawyers need to learn lessons from both. By trying to understand why things happened as they did, protégés can more clearly see where they have come from and where they need to go.

A great deal of lawyering is learned by surmounting challenging assignments and difficult professional problems. Mentors do associates no favors by protecting them from such challenges. Instead, mentors should help protégés learn and grow professionally by setting high standards and encouraging protégés to tackle challenges head-on.

Assignments that require protégés to stretch beyond their comfort level are among the most effective career-building events. But mentors need to be sensitive to a protégé's readiness. While work that is too easy will offer little learning, experiences that are too difficult may lead to setbacks, including a loss of confidence. Mentors should praise and reinforce successes and be sure to offer support when things do not go as well as had been hoped.

Modeling. Mentoring is in large part based on modeling. Young lawyers who are trying to develop their own professional style and identity frequently look to mentors as role models. Consequently, mentors should be aware that less experienced lawyers are observing them and "trying on" their attitudes and behaviors "to see how they fit." Attitudes and behaviors may be rejected or accepted, but they will have an impact on the protégé.

A mentor's actions have a far greater influence on a protégé than what the mentor says. Protégés observe, imitate, and learn what the firm really wants by emulating the lawyers they see. Mentors should try to model positive professional and interpersonal behaviors by bringing enthusiasm and a positive attitude to the mentoring relationship. It is important that mentors' behavior be consistent with their own values and those of the firm. For example, mentors who emphasize the importance of teamwork for great client service should treat others working on client matters as a team. A mentor who espouses teamwork but withholds case-related information from others on the team sends out inconsistent signals and loses credibility.

Mentoring is not a cloning process; good mentors expect and encourage protégés to develop their own practice styles and approaches, not to simply replicate the mentor's. Effective mentors appreciate a protégé's strengths, talents, and unique attributes, and look for opportunities to make the most of them.

Confidence building. A mentor can play a pivotal role in helping a protégé develop self-confidence. Lawyers work hard under stressful, demanding conditions in an adversarial system that can be rough and mean. Most young lawyers experience periods of anxiety, frustration, and disillusionment about their work. Even the most outstanding lawyers have moments of self-doubt. Through words and gestures of support that demonstrate faith in the protégé, mentors build the protégé's self-esteem. Novice lawyers often feel highly vulnerable; they fear being found inadequate or lacking. They look to mentors who have been through the same developmental process for encouragement. Mentors provide that encouragement by affirming the validity of their protégés' concerns, reminding them of their strengths, and letting them know they are okay where they are.

Mentors can be especially valuable when things go awry. When protégés take reasonable risks or make considered decisions in the face of uncertainty and pressure, mentors should commend the protégés' actions, even if they fail. Mentors can also help protégés analyze why things did not turn out well and what might lead to a better outcome next time. When protégés take risks that are too great, stretch themselves too far, or make poor decisions, mentors can help them understand, correct, and learn from their mistakes. Instead of forgiving or repairing a protégé's error, mentors should offer emotional support, repair battered self-esteem, and encourage protégés to pick themselves up and keep on moving. Mentors who are willing to share stories of their own less-than-successful experiences can make the protégé's recovery easier; it can be reassuring to learn that an admired mentor has occasionally stumbled. This emotional support and guidance can turn a feeling of miserable failure into a confidence-building experience. It is one of the many ways a mentor can let protégés know that the mentor still has confidence in them. Protégés grow to believe in themselves when they know their mentor believes in them.

Mentors also build confidence by advocating for their protégés. Because mentors get to know protégés well and have a stake in the protégé's success, they are naturally positioned to take on the role of promoting the protégé's interests. As protégés advance professionally, mentors can act as champions to promote them within the organization, especially as they approach partnership or other promotion points. Mentors can also introduce protégés to other people who can help their careers and open doors to important committees, outside organizations, and clients.

Coaching. Coaching is a process for improving performance. In the mentoring context, coaching focuses on the protégé's effort to set and attain development and career goals, marshal the resources needed to attain those goals, and identify the obstacles that stand in the way. Unlike ordinary feedback and performance reviews, which are retrospective, coaching is prospective. It looks not just at past and current performance but also at future growth and development. Once a plan is in place, the mentor monitors the individual's progress and tries to keep up both momentum and morale. Along the way, mentors can help minimize or eliminate obstacles, arrange opportunities and introductions, and offer advice and guidance. If, for example, a protégé needs to improve client relation skills, a mentor can advise the protégé about how to work with clients and suggest (or even sponsor the protégé for) assignments or activities where the protégé can practice and learn these skills.

The mentor's coaching role is also important in helping the protégé process feedback from managers and supervisors. Mentors give protégés constructive, direct, and honest feedback on the work assignments they supervise. In addition, they can help the protégé turn the feedback from yearly performance reviews into specific performance goals by translating the comments and suggestions made during the review. If the protégé trusts the mentor and values the mentor's opinions, then this feedback — and especially the mentor's criticism — will be taken more seriously and constructively. In this way, mentors reduce the protégé's emotional reactions or disappointments and help the protégé maintain a clearer, more positive perspective on what and how they need to improve.

One of the most effective coaching tools is inquiry, i.e., helping protégés learn by asking them questions. Like the Socratic method used in law schools, inquiry induces the learner to think through and analyze a situation. It asks protégés to identify the results they want to work for, to assess their own performance, and to decide what steps they will take to move ahead. Instead of instructing protégés how to handle assignments, or "rescuing" them from mistakes or difficult situations, mentors can use inquiry to help protégés find their own way. Learning will be more powerful when protégés find insights and answers for themselves.

Counseling. Mentors are a primary source of information and advice about career-related issues. Legal careers can be difficult and frustrating, filled with treacherous obstacles and pitfalls along the road to success. Especially in their early years of practice, lawyers long for someone they can discuss these issues with and can go to for career advice. They may have career doubts or special ambitions, a desire to change practice areas or to take a detour off the conventional partnership track. Mentors can offer advice and help protégés find solutions to these career-related problems. Mentors cannot solve their protégés' problems but they can help their protégés learn how to find their own solutions and make sound career decisions. Rather than fixing the road, mentors help protégés become more competent at navigating around the potholes.

Mentors are positioned to offer this counsel because they have the big picture in view. They look at the protégé's career in a context broader than a particular assignment or performance review period. They try to see the issues through the protégé's eyes, but mentors also have the advantage of experience. Moreover, from their positions in the organization, mentors know what the organization expects from its lawyers. This combined perspective gives the mentor an ideal vantage point from which to counsel protégés on career issues.

But the mentor must be cautious. This very perspective may tempt the mentor to try to set goals for the protégé. The mentoring process, however, is best served when protégés decide their own career goals. Good mentors help protégés develop a career strategy that will lead to success as the protégé defines success. In addition, a mentor's willingness to help protégés clarify their own professional interests and goals may be tested if the protégé's interests conflict with the mentor's. When the mentor's and protégé's interests collide, both need to recognize that any advice the mentor offers may be less than objective. For instance, when Doug told Allan, his mentor, that he wanted to cut back on his work hours for several months, Allan advised Doug that this would be a bad career move because the firm would question his commitment. When Allan thought about it more, he realized that his real concern was for himself. Allan depended on Doug to handle several client matters for him, and Doug was one of Allan's best associates. Allan had no doubt that Doug was committed to the firm and would continue to work hard for Allan's clients even if he worked fewer hours. So Allan changed his advice and told Doug he would support the request for reduced hours.

■ KEY PRACTICES OF PROTÉGÉS

Initiative. Employers provide work, training, and resources to help develop lawyering skills, but the ultimate responsibility for professional development rests with the protégé. Many young lawyers who want a mentor's help do not realize how much they can do to start and influence the mentoring relationship. Rather than wait to be chosen by a mentor, prospective protégés should take the initiative. Lawyers who sit before their keyboards hoping someone will notice the high quality of their work are less likely to be mentored than those who ask potential mentors for advice and feedback. Even when assigned a mentor, protégés should show initiative in the mentoring relationship. Unless the mentor says otherwise, protégés need not wait to be called. Make the first move; show the mentor your enthusiasm.

If the firm does not assign mentors, lawyers need to go out and find mentors on their own. Mentoring relationships usually develop naturally as lawyers work together. Most of the time they happen serendipitously, when two people are drawn to each other professionally. But smart lawyers take the initiative to create conditions that lead to serendipity. (See "Finding a Mentor" earlier in this chapter.)

Goal setting. Mary Cranston, who in 1999 became the first woman to chair Pillsbury, Madison & Sutro, LLP, attributes much of her success to envisioning goals for herself early in her career and making day-to-day decisions that moved her toward her vision. When working with a mentor, protégés, too, should establish career goals and adopt strategies to achieve their goals. Those goals may be long-term (e.g., building a reputation as a First Amendment expert) or short-term (e.g., improving negotiation skills), and they need not be fixed and immutable. To the contrary, the hallmark of a successful career plan is flexibility: the ability to recognize and respond to new opportunities when they arise. When needs change, goals and strategies will have to change to accommodate them, and the protégé may need to find different mentors. Finding the right mentors for changing needs is a key factor in achieving a career plan. When protégés know what they hope to gain, they can look for the person in the best position to help them. The value of goals in mentoring is that they help the parties focus on what the protégé wants to get out of a mentoring experience. Clear goals and expectations make mentoring relationships more effective.

Receptivity. Protégés should seek and welcome the mentor's feedback. They should recognize that a mentor's criticism and recommendations are intended to promote the protégé's professional growth. Mentors who take a serious interest in their protégés' development frequently offer advice on sensitive subjects. These subjects may include matters that the protégé considers personal (e.g., how to dress for the office), insignificant (e.g., how to work with a legal assistant), or extremely important (e.g., how to promote oneself to the firm's partners). Protégés need not accept all the suggestions or feedback they receive from a mentor, but they should respect the mentor's advice, even when disagreeing with it. Protégés who take personal offense at the mentor's criticism or suggestions for improvement will not be able to enjoy the developmental benefits of the mentoring relationship.

Worthiness. To be a protégé is to be someone whom others want to mentor. Most mentors will invest time and energy only in someone they think will succeed. Protégés who are perceived as competent attract more mentors and those mentors provide more career and psychosocial mentoring functions. Mentors identify promising protégés on the basis of demonstrated potential for growth and development. There are many ways that lawyers can demonstrate this potential, and some behaviors and qualities will appeal more to one mentor than another. In general, traits that mentors want to see in potential protégés include:

- Intelligence;
- Openness to ideas, feedback, and guidance;
- Listening skills;
- Interpersonal skills;
- Outgoing personalities;
- Ambition and determination;
- Technical skills;
- Commitment to client service;
- Integrity;
- Accountability;
- Loyalty; and
- The ability to complete a project.

Mentors prefer to work with lawyers who have a positive attitude, are committed to workplace goals, learn quickly, and demonstrate the drive to achieve professional success. This requires junior lawyers to be congenial and upbeat in attending to work; to build a reputation for working hard and doing excellent work; and to make themselves visible through high-profile assignments and committees. It is easier to find mentors when you are recognized as a lawyer with great promise.

When lawyers are new to practice, mentors expect them to put in long hours and produce work that is thorough, thoughtful, accurate, and on point. At this and every career stage, the protégé's legal skills must be solid. To be perceived as worthy as time goes on, however, a protégé has to move beyond those expectations; it becomes necessary to "think like an owner." This means that protégés must look at law practice not from the perspective of someone who only does what they are told (no matter how well they do it), but as if they were in charge of the case, the client, and the firm. In addition, partners expect protégés to continually increase their business literacy — i.e., their familiarity with the client's business and the business aspects of law. Let mentors see that you are trying to do these things and how your efforts will ultimately benefit them and the firm. Let them see that you enjoy your work and have a strong desire to move ahead. When they see your enthusiasm, motivation, and maturation, they will be eager to help you.

Appreciation. Because mentors are interested in their protégés' careers, it is especially important for protégés to keep mentors informed about their progress and about how the mentor contributed to that progress. Good mentors genuinely care about their protégés and what happens to them. Since they have invested themselves in the protégé's career, they want to know if their effort was worthwhile. Most importantly, protégés should always thank their mentors, in words and in deeds.

The importance of showing appreciation to mentors cannot be overestimated. Hastings College of the Law has an Alumni Mentor Program in which volunteer alumni serve as mentors to law students. One mentor in the program worked with a third-year law student who was diagnosed with cancer during the mentoring period and died shortly after passing the bar exam. Before she died, the young woman wrote to her mentor, thanking him and expressing her appreciation for his help. She also encouraged him to continue being a mentor to others: "I do hope you will continue to participate in the mentor program; you've been a great resource to me. Had things turned out differently, I would have felt like I could turn to you for advice long after I found my first job." Although this tragic experience was his first mentoring relationship, the mentor was inspired to continue volunteering as a mentor in the Hastings program.[1]

The impact of expressed gratitude can also result in tangible rewards, as the following example shows. A group of employees working for a government contractor in Washington managed to get through a very tense and difficult period thanks to extraordinary help from their supervisor, Mac. The employees sent an unsolicited letter to the company that included the following paragraph:

> "Mac has had to handle many problems stemming from the recent crisis, but his many responsibilities have not prevented him from doing what he does best: mentoring his team and keeping the office a fun place to work. Mac always makes time to help us and responds quickly to our needs, regardless of how busy he might be. He manages us with a never-ending supply of patience, guidance, and enthusiasm, while still maintaining control of a large volume of work."

As a result of that letter, Mac received an extra and unexpected bonus.

CONCLUDING MENTORING RELATIONSHIPS

Unless the mentor and protégé have agreed to a definite term for their relationship, most informal mentoring relationships tend to reach a natural conclusion when the parties' objectives are met or as the relationship evolves. Over time, the circumstances and needs of the parties change. The protégé becomes proficient and establishes a strong professional identity. The protégé no longer needs as much from the mentor. The mentoring relationship does not play the central role it played earlier, and the protégé becomes more of an equal to the

---

[1] "A Graduate's Legacy: On the Importance of Mentoring," *Hastings Community*, Summer 1999.

mentor. At this stage, the relationship between mentor and protégé may end. However, if there is still a close affinity and mutual respect, a new kind of relationship will form, and the mentor and protégé will remain close colleagues and possibly close friends.

Not all mentoring relationships end so smoothly. The change from a mentor-protégé relationship to a relationship of equals may cause mixed feelings. Some lawyers have a hard time letting go after the mentoring relationship has run its course; separation involves loss. Mentors fear losing the influence they have over the protégé's development and career. Protégés are afraid to let go because they will lose the comfort and security they receive from their mentors.

If we look at the mentoring process as a journey, the protégé walks behind the mentor at the beginning, watching, learning, and following; gradually, as the protégé's development progresses, the two walk side by side. In some cases, the protégé may actually surpass the mentor in terms of professional achievement and stature. Most mentors take satisfaction in the advancement and success of their protégés. But sometimes mentors become jealous of their protégés' success and may even compete with them bitterly over clients and recognition.

When mentoring relationships conclude positively, protégés move on and take favorable memories with them. Long after the relationship ends, they may deal with a new situation by thinking about how their mentor would have handled it. They also model themselves after their mentor when they become mentors to others. Mentors also move on, taking pride in the people they mentor and keeping track of their career progress. Even when time and distance separates mentors and protégés, the impact of their mentoring relationship endures.

CHAPTER 6

NECESSARY ELEMENTS OF A MENTORING PROGRAM

"[I]nfluence follows along lines of affiliation and contact."

DEBORAH TANNEN

Most lawyers would prefer to have a mentoring relationship develop naturally rather than through a formal program. Research confirms that informal mentoring relationships are more effective and comprehensive than those which are planned or assigned because the parties like each other and are highly motivated from the outset.[1] Because such relationships are rare, more and more law firms have begun to implement formal mentoring programs to ensure that the benefits of mentoring are more widely available. These programs plan and assign mentoring relationships and are used deliberately to enhance work skills, knowledge, cultural integration, and career progress. When carefully designed, explained, and managed, formal programs can provide an excellent mentoring experience for mentors and associates alike.

Some legal employers shy away from formal mentoring programs, convinced that because mentoring relationships are personal they cannot be created by assignment. Others have tried mentoring programs that started off with good intentions but went nowhere. As a result, many lawyers have been promised mentoring relationships that never materialized. The NALP Foundation's *Keeping the Keepers* study

---

[1] See Mullen and Chao in the References at the conclusion of this book.

found that associates were "almost unanimous in their negative assessment" of formal programs, feeling that these programs never seemed to work. Associates recommended that law firms develop informal and flexible mentoring systems instead.

Contrary to these negative perceptions, formal mentoring programs can and do work. A mentoring program is simply an organized mentoring effort sponsored by a firm to systematically promote the professional development of a targeted group of lawyers. Because mentors and protégés are matched by the firm, the mentoring relationships that are created are *formal*, as distinguished from *informal* mentoring relationships that arise naturally in the workplace. The lawyers targeted for mentoring may be all the lawyers in the firm or a subset of them, such as new associates or lateral hires. Rather than leave mentoring to chance, a formal program tries to promote and facilitate effective mentoring by creating mentoring relationships between pairs or small groups of willing participants and providing the training, resources, and support needed to reinforce their mentoring efforts.

Although lawyers' negativity toward mentoring programs is understandable, the reality is that most law firms cannot rely on lawyers to provide mentoring informally. Programs can and should be flexible, but some structural elements are necessary to ensure that mentoring occurs. Without a formal program, most lawyers face too many competing demands and priorities, and too few rewards, to act as mentors. Without a formal program, a few associates may have excellent mentoring relationships, but most associates will have none.

Organizations that are committed to mentoring and invest the resources necessary to design, implement, and sustain formal mentoring programs have shown that they can be highly successful systems to train, develop, advance, and retain talented employees. Mentoring programs operate successfully in the business world, education, government, community services, and other professions. Of the companies listed in the 1999 *Fortune Magazine*'s "100 Best Companies to Work For," 60 percent had mentoring programs. But success requires planning, commitment, and training. These next few chapters provide guidance for legal employers who have the desire and the will to ensure that their lawyers experience the powerful benefits of mentoring.

This chapter will discuss the ten elements necessary for an effective program. (See *Table 4* on the following page.) As we begin, let me raise a word of caution. In designing a mentoring program, it is possible to

TABLE 4. NECESSARY ELEMENTS OF A MENTORING PROGRAM

- Leadership's commitment
- Clearly articulated program objectives
- Program parameters
  - Voluntary participation
  - Duration of mentoring assignment
  - Time commitment
  - Scope of the relationship
  - Budget
- Procedure and criteria for matching mentors and associates
- A program coordinator
- Training
- Ongoing support and program monitoring
- Evaluation
- Written guidelines
- Incentives for mentoring

become so enamored of the structural components that you lose sight of the intended result: meaningful mentoring relationships. These mentoring relationships should be exciting and dynamic, with all participants deriving benefits and satisfaction. The purpose of providing a structure is to allow mentoring to happen. The program design should facilitate and support mentoring relationships, not dictate or control them. Don't worry about designing a perfect program or a single model of mentoring. So long as you have the necessary elements, your program will succeed.

LEADERSHIP'S COMMITMENT

The most critical ingredient for a successful mentoring program is the commitment of your firm's leadership. No matter how good your intentions are, if the firm is not fully committed to the program, the entire effort will be wasted. This means you must have unwavering support from the top, not just a pronouncement as the program gets under way that "henceforth, we will all be mentors." Your firm leaders have to support the changes needed to create an environment where the mentoring program can and will thrive. To do this, firm leaders must work to achieve consensus within the firm about the importance of mentoring, and they must actively participate in the program by becoming mentoring role models for the other lawyers in the firm.

If your firm agrees that mentoring is a major firm priority, lawyers should be held accountable to that standard. Whether or not they participate in the formal program, all partners who supervise associates should be expected to do some mentoring, and they should be invited to training programs that teach mentoring skills. While the firm should not penalize partners who decline to be formal mentors, behavior that is contrary to the norms of good mentoring should not be tolerated. A firm that is seriously committed to mentoring would not condone behavior like Elizabeth's. Elizabeth is a very busy partner and successful rainmaker, but she has little patience or regard for associates. When junior associates ask her questions about assignments that she has given them, she snaps at them, saying: "Don't expect me to give you answers. This is a sink or swim firm, and if you can't make it, get out before you go under." If the associates make mistakes, Elizabeth blames them — loudly — and makes them feel stupid. This has caused several associates to leave the firm. A firm that is committed to mentoring and associate development would not allow this behavior to continue. It would hold Elizabeth accountable in a tangible and significant way.

CLEARLY ARTICULATED PROGRAM OBJECTIVES

The first step in establishing a mentoring program is to determine the program's purpose. After you articulate what the program is intended to achieve, you can set specific objectives and design the program to meet those objectives.

A mentoring program should be designed to maximize the potential of the firm's most valuable resource, its lawyers. The beauty of mentoring is that it aligns the interests of the firm and its individual lawyers: both benefit when lawyers are proficient, productive, and happy. This is true from both a professional and a business standpoint. In addition to planning how your mentoring program will further the professional interests of your attorneys, consider how the program will fit into your firm's business goals and strategy. Every mentoring program should address the law firm's business interests. Specific business reasons for having a mentoring program will, of course, vary from firm to firm.

When your purpose is clearly articulated, the desired outcomes of your mentoring program should be stated as program objectives. Objectives must identify both the attorneys to be mentored and the intended benefits of the mentoring relationship. They must be specific, realistic, and measurable. Specificity enables all participants to understand exactly what the program hopes to accomplish. Realism is an element that is often overlooked in the fervent desire to set up a program. Measurability is necessary in order to assess whether your mentoring program accomplishes your objectives.

Articulating program objectives will keep your purpose clear and facilitate program evaluation. If you don't know what you hope your program will achieve, you cannot decide the best way to proceed, and, later, you cannot determine whether your objectives are being met. For example, many mentoring programs are responses to a high rate of associate turnover. If this is your firm's motivation, the overall purpose of your mentoring program would be to reduce associate attrition. Objectives would be directed at alleviating the specific causes of attrition. The same objectives might apply to all associates in the

---

TABLE 5. EXAMPLES OF MENTORING PROGRAM OBJECTIVES

For a program designed to help get <u>new associates</u> off to a good start in the firm and in practice, objectives might be to:

- introduce new associates to everyone on their floor and in their practice group
- ease their transition to law practice through orientation and training programs
- provide detailed information about the firm's lawyers and areas of practice
- foster professional relationships with other associates through mentor-protégé social events
- provide opportunities for interaction with partners in small group lunches

For a program designed to prepare <u>senior associates</u> for partnership, objectives might be to:

- place senior associates on key firm committees
- help them build strong client relationships
- provide guidance and opportunities for business development
- increase their contact with partners within and outside of their practice area
- provide access to firm leaders through monthly business meetings

---

program, or your program might encompass different objectives for different groups of associates. If you have determined that the principal cause of attrition among second-year associates is lack of client contact, your objective would be to increase the client responsibilities that partners give to those associates. If the principal cause of turnover for fifth-year associates is lack of courtroom experience, the objective would be for mentors to get those associates into court.

Mentoring program objectives can respond to a short-term need such as the arrival of summer associates, but most mentoring programs are strategic — i.e., they are intended to promote the long-term health of the firm. *Table 5* lists examples of objectives for mentoring programs. Whether your program has one objective or many, be sure all the objectives are spelled out clearly so that everyone understands what the program will and will not do. If the objectives are misunderstood, people may have unrealistic expectations, which will frustrate participants and cause the program to fail.

PROGRAM PARAMETERS

Voluntary participation. Because it involves a personal relationship, mentoring must be voluntary. A program can facilitate mentoring but it cannot legislate that mentoring shall occur. Lawyers who are unwilling to make the necessary commitment freely and voluntarily should be permitted to decline. Lawyers who object to being either mentors or protégés should not be forced to participate or penalized for refusing. Similarly, lawyers who drop out of the program should be free to do so without penalty.

Duration of mentoring assignments. The duration of mentoring assignments depends on the objectives of the program. Consider how long it will realistically take for mentors and associates to achieve those objectives. The assigned relationships can then conclude at the end of the agreed upon term. This will make it easier for participants whose formal mentoring relationships have run their course to leave the relationship gracefully and naturally. If some assigned mentoring pairs wish to continue beyond the formal time period set by the program, by all means encourage them to do so. When a mentor and assigned associate find value in the mentoring relationship and continue on an informal mentoring basis, consider it to be a sign of the success of both your matching efforts and the program overall.

As a general rule, try to keep assigned relationships short; make them only long enough to meet specific mentoring objectives. An orientation program for new associates is a good example of a program that may need only short-term mentoring assignments. If mentors in the program are merely expected to acculturate new lawyers to the firm, a six-month relationship may be sufficient. On the other hand, a program devoted to career planning requires at least a year or more.

Time commitment. It is imperative that time expectations be clearly limited. Lawyers have very little free time for anything. As one harried law firm partner exclaimed, "I don't have time to be a mentor! If anyone else does I suspect they're not getting their work done or they're not bringing in clients." When you add mentoring obligations to an overloaded schedule, most lawyers will recoil — and many will rebel. Mentoring does take time, but a great deal of mentoring happens while the mentor and protégé are working together. Lawyers ought to look for mentoring opportunities in every assignment and every work encounter. Many important lessons are taught quickly by explaining why certain terms were omitted from a deal and other terms were included; telling an associate that the client was pleased with her work — and why; or inviting an associate to observe and listen while you handle a thorny problem in a conference call. These things do not take long, but they communicate to the associate a vital message: that you want that associate to learn and grow. Studies have shown that in formal mentoring relationships, the amount of time spent together counts less than the quality of the interactions between mentor and protégé.[1]

Because of the mistaken belief that mentoring requires a huge amount of time, it arouses anxiety in people who under other circumstances might really enjoy helping someone become a better lawyer. To dispel this anxiety, give mentoring participants an idea of the time they should spend in mentoring activities. Some firms set a specific time requirement (e.g., "mentors and associates should meet one hour per week"), while others prefer to leave the mentor and associate free to

---

[1] Ellen J. Mullen, "Vocational and Psychosocial Mentoring Functions: Identifying Mentors Who Serve Both," *Human Resources Development Quarterly*, Vol. 9, No. 4, Winter 1998.

decide. In most cases, mentoring pairs can stay in touch by telephone and email, with periodic face-to-face meetings over lunch or a cup of coffee. The whole process might amount to just an hour or two per month to discuss mentoring objectives — not a huge burden at all.

Some firms budget time for mentoring, i.e., they "deposit" a certain number of hours into a "mentoring bank" or a billing category that enables — and encourages — lawyers to invest time in mentoring. These hours are usually classified as something other than billable or non-billable time.

Although most mentoring does not require an inordinate amount of time, one significant exception is in the area of legal writing. A mentor who works with an associate on improving writing skills should be prepared to devote a substantial amount of time. Editing, explaining, and giving feedback on legal writing is very time intensive. Unless you have lawyers who enjoy and want to do this kind of work, your firm might be better served carving writing skills out of the mentoring program. Instead, use legal writing classes or hire a writing coach to provide one-on-one assistance when needed.

Scope of the relationship. In most law firm mentoring programs, mentoring relationships are intended to be social (e.g., for orientation) or developmental (i.e., to address one or more of the associate's professional development needs). Some associates may also want help with personal issues, such as deciding when to have children or how to manage personal relationships when work is very stressful. In many mentoring relationships, mentor and associate are comfortable treating personal issues as natural extensions of professional ones. But some lawyers who are capable mentors when the subject is skills development feel uneasy or unwilling to discuss an associate's personal problems. Mentors who are uncomfortable or embarrassed by an associate's shared intimacy may pull back from the mentoring relationship.

To avoid this situation, the mentor and associate should understand at the onset whether personal matters are within the scope of their mentoring relationship. They should be cautioned that private or intimate concerns should not be raised unless both parties clearly signal a willingness to discuss them. Your program guidelines can limit the kinds of professional issues to be addressed, or you can leave it up to the mentor and protégé to decide for themselves what they will and will not cover. Each mentoring relationship will vary, based on the participants' styles, strengths, and needs, and the goals they agree to undertake in the relationship.

Budget. Give mentors a budget to cover mentoring activities, especially if your mentoring program expects mentors to entertain associates. Where entertainment is expected, as in a program intended to socialize new or lateral associates, explain how the activities will be financed and the type of expenses that are permitted. This is especially important if your mentors are not partners. Better yet, set up an account which specifically earmarks money for mentoring, and tell mentors what they can spend on mentoring activities.

PROCEDURE AND CRITERIA FOR MATCHING MENTORS AND ASSOCIATES

In a mentoring program, the firm assigns a mentor to each participating associate. The firm may permit program participants to select individuals with whom they would like to be matched, but the final decisions are usually made by the firm, not the individuals. Assigned mentoring relationships have been likened to an arranged marriage. You hope the individuals will find true love, but the odds are against them. Matching people poses tricky challenges and risks whether you match them randomly or use elaborate criteria. Occasionally you will make a brilliant match, sometimes the match won't work out at all, but usually your matched pairs will do a satisfactory job of working toward their objectives.

The principle of matching is simple: you want the mentoring pair to promote the associate's development and achieve the firm's program objectives. Keep in mind that you are not arranging a lifetime relationship. You are pairing people up to achieve specific, well-defined goals for a set period of time. A broader, deeper friendship may develop for some, but that is not the purpose or objective of your mentoring program.

The firm can conduct the actual process of matching in many ways (see "Matching Methods" on the opposite page). The principal distinction is whether or not the firm will offer participants a chance to state their preferred mentor or protégé. The size of your firm, the firm's culture and traditions, the number of lawyers in the program, the

MATCHING METHODS

Participants state preferences, firm decides.
1. Mentors and associates choose.
2. Mentors choose.
3. Associates choose.

Firm decides without participant input.
4. Firm matches based on similarities.
5. Firm matches based on differences.
6. Firm matches randomly.

personalities of those lawyers, and a host of other factors will dictate the particular approach that is best for your firm.

Although the firm makes the ultimate decisions, mentoring is most effective when both participants can select their mentoring partners. Some firms allow mentors, associates, or both to select their preferred match. However, when it is unfeasible or inadvisable for lawyers to do so, the firm matches mentors and protégés. Some firms match on the basis of similarities while others prefer to match people who have little in common but much to offer each other.

Matching by Participant's Choice. It is best to design as much lawyer choice as possible into your matching process. Matching people who have selected one another increases the chances of a successful match. If the associates you are matching have been in the firm for a period of time or are known through your summer program, mentors and associates may be able to choose each other. People will work better together in a planned mentoring relationship when the match feels natural and comfortable. If you match people who already have a positive regard for each other, the relationship will seem a little more spontaneous and not feel "forced."

Begin by determining the preferences of associates and potential mentors. Send each associate in the program a list of the lawyers who are available as mentors and send each potential mentor a list of available associates. Ask each group to nominate three of four lawyers with whom they would like to be matched. Alternatively, allow either mentors or associates (but not both) to choose. At New York's Fried, Frank, Harris, Shriver & Jacobson, which assigns two associate advisors and one partner mentor to each incoming associate, associates are asked what characteristics they would like their mentors to have, and the firm then tries to find a suitable match based on preferences and interests.

Firms that ask participants to choose or characterize their preferred mentors or associates should try to honor the lawyers' preferences, taking into account the associate's needs, the mentor's abilities, and the firm's objectives. Sometimes the firm may decide that a requested match is inadvisable or that a better match exists. In those cases, the firm might believe that the associate's professional development, the firm's business goals, or the mentoring program objectives would best be served by matching two lawyers who have not selected each other. Specific countervailing reasons not to make a requested match include the following:

- The mentor is unable to help with the associate's general developmental needs;

- The mentor is having problems that may be unknown to the associate but may harm the associate's experience or career in the firm;

- The mentor will be unavailable during a large part of the mentoring program cycle;

- The mentor has been unreliable or ineffective as a mentor in the past;

- The associate has special needs (e.g., poor management skills) best met by another mentor;

- An associate has worked a lot with the requested mentor and needs exposure to more partners or a different kind of work.

The fact that two attorneys who request each other are not matched in the mentoring program does not mean they cannot have a mentoring relationship. To the contrary, they should be encouraged to pursue informal mentoring. The associate will then be fortunate to have two mentors.

Matching by firm criteria. If matches are not based on participants' choices, the firm has to decide what criteria it will use to pair people up. Your goal is to promote both the associate's professional development and the firm's program objectives. It is important to try to match people with compatible personalities and work styles, although their background, interests, and experience can be similar or very different.

It is usually easier for two people to start a relationship when they have a lot in common, such as shared background, beliefs, or personal interests. Your objective is not to match people who are identical but rather to find people with enough common basis to serve as the starting point of a relationship. All the lawyers in your firm share some professional interests that they can build on. They all have a common interest in the law, the firm, and, through your mentoring program, in associates' development.

On the other hand, your mentors and associates may not have a lot in common, or the firm may decide that program objectives will be best served by deliberately pairing lawyers of contrasting backgrounds, perspectives, and life experiences. This is often the case in corporate mentoring programs where lawyers are paired with mentors or protégés from other departments. (See Chapter Eleven.)

Random matching. Some firms may prefer a more random matching process, pairing associates to mentors without close analysis or set criteria. Lawyers may be matched in any number of ways — e.g., alphabetically, by office proximity, or on the basis of work assignments. This may be all that a small firm or practice group needs for effective matches.

■ RACE AND ETHNICITY CONSIDERATIONS IN MENTOR ASSIGNMENTS

The elements of race and ethnicity raise vexing questions for a mentoring program.[1] The overriding purpose of any mentoring program is to give associates a meaningful and worthwhile mentoring experience. As with other associates, minority lawyers should be given a chance to express their choices for a mentor. Some minority associates may feel that they can only have a meaningful mentoring relationship with mentors from the same minority group. But it may not always be possible to make these matches, and it may not be in the associates' best interests to do so.

Race or ethnicity may be one consideration in matching but should not be the only factor. People who share the same racial or

---

[1] See Ragins and Abbott in the References at the conclusion of this book.

cultural background have a basis for connecting that allows trust to build more readily. When they meet, they assume they have a shared life experience on the basis of their common race or culture. Minority lawyers often feel emotions and insecurities that may seem strange or hypersensitive to someone who has not had the same life experiences. A mentor from the same minority group understands those feelings immediately and without explanation. This shared experience and understanding create a comfort level that makes a relationship develop more easily. When associates feel very strongly that they need mentors from the same minority group, the firm should try to accommodate them in some way. Two very effective approaches are through peer and group mentoring. (See Chapter Ten.)

Nonetheless, it is not always possible to match associates with mentors from the same minority group. Nor is it always advisable. When mentors and associates are paired strictly by race or culture, they may be perceived as "separate" from the rest of the firm. This reinforces their status as "outsiders" and undermines their efforts to be fully accepted into the firm. It also expects too much of minority mentors. It forces them to devote a great deal of time to minority associates, while it limits the time they have to spend with other associates. This restricts their exposure to and influence over majority lawyers in the firm. Moreover, pairing associates with mentors from the same minority group deprives minority associates of good non-minority mentors in the firm. The firm may have excellent non-minority mentors who are sensitive to minority attorneys' concerns and would give minority associates superb mentoring experiences.

It may be more important in a mentoring program to match people from different backgrounds so that they can learn from and about each other. When matching minority attorneys, what is important is that the mentor and associate be willing to accept each other's gender, racial, cultural, or other differences and appreciate how those differences may have affected their lives. So long as their personalities are compatible and their differences do not create conflict or interfere with the mentoring process, the differences between the mentor and associate may actually enrich the mentoring relationship. As they begin to understand and appreciate their differences, the mentoring experience can become more profound for them. Existing cultural barriers in the firm come down and diversity becomes the norm.

■ GENDER, SEX, AND ROMANTIC ENTANGLEMENTS

Millions of men and women work together daily without getting romantically involved. However, in formal mentoring relationships, gender differences can cause thorny complications. In your program, you are pairing people up for a relationship that is expected to be trusting and intimate. In most of these relationships, the mentor will hold a position of power over the associate. If one or both of the mentoring pair becomes attracted to the other, the combination of intimacy, power, and sexual attraction can have explosive consequences.

Mentors and associates often work very closely and under a lot of pressure. In their work, they may travel together, work late at night and on weekends, and experience a great deal of excitement and stress. As they grow to respect and admire each other, the relationship may become personal as well as professional. If they are attracted to each other, it may also become romantic and sexual. Sex and romance will inevitably occur from time to time, with or without a mentoring program. You cannot prevent people from being sexually attracted to one another and you cannot stop them from becoming romantically involved.

Cross-gender issues are present when women are mentors to male associates, but because most senior lawyers are men, the odds are pretty good that most mentors in your program will be men. Many of those men will be wary of being in a mentoring relationship with someone of the opposite sex. They fear that their innocent actions or comments might be misconstrued and that they might be falsely accused of sexual impropriety or even harassment. As a result, many men refrain from mentoring women. These fears should not be honored, but neither should they be ignored.

Women face a somewhat different problem. When women and men have close mentoring relationships, office gossip may spread rumors of a romance. Regardless of how the rumors portray the man in the purported relationship, the woman is inevitably painted in an unfavorable light. For instance, people may whisper that a successful woman was promoted in return for sexual favors. When Anne was an associate in a large New York law firm, she became a protégé of Grant, a powerful securities lawyer in the same firm. Anne was an outstanding lawyer with a solid book of business and her capability had never been questioned. Shortly after Anne was made a partner, rumors began to circulate that she was romantically involved with Grant. Although the rumors were untrue, comments about how she had "slept her way to the top" surfaced years later when a rival tried to prevent her appointment to the firm's Management Committee.

Sexual relationships between associates and mentors, as with associates and any supervising partner, should be discouraged. Your program can deal with issues of sex and romance preventively by raising participants' awareness of the ramifications. Discuss gender-related issues in your orientation and training programs. Let people know what they can do if they are attracted to each other but are not yet romantically involved, and what they can and should do if they do become involved. Discuss these steps, along with the risks and potentially destructive aspects of office romance, within the context of your firm's policy on sexual harassment. That discussion should explain the procedures to follow, and the resources available, when either the associate or mentor wants guidance, needs reassignment, or believes someone has behaved inappropriately.

■ MAKING THE MATCHES

Responsibility for the matching process usually rests with the mentoring program coordinator, although the matches may be decided by another designated person or a committee. Unless your firm takes the random selection route, the matching process must be handled carefully by people who are most familiar with the associates and mentors. For new associates, this would most likely include your recruiting director, members of the hiring committee, and the people who run your summer program. Others who might be involved include practice group leaders or department heads, and lawyers, administrators, or staff who introduced an associate to the firm or participated in the recruitment process.

If the people doing the matching are familiar with the mentors and associates, they may have sufficient knowledge of associates' needs, and of all participants' personalities, work styles, backgrounds, and interests to make effective matches. For associates who have gone through at least one evaluation process in the firm, or who have self-identified special developmental needs, input regarding the associate's evaluation will enable you to match the associate with a mentor best suited to address those needs. If your information about participants is not sufficient to make good matches, supplement what you know through questionnaires, interviews with participants, and input from others in the firm. You can ask about any professional, developmental, or personal factors that may contribute to the formation of a mentoring relationship, including:

- Developmental needs;

- Professional goals;

- Practice areas;

- Mentor's expertise;

- Substantive legal interests;

- Business or industry experience;

- Memberships in organizations;

- Colleges or law schools attended;

- Undergraduate majors; and

- Hobbies.

Mentors must be consulted before any matches are announced. No assignment should ever be made to an unwilling mentor. If the proposed mentor says no, make a reassignment before the matches become public. Associates, too, must accept their assigned mentor if the relationship is to succeed. If your matching process allows associates to choose their mentors, you should also confer in advance with any associates who will not be matched with the mentor they selected. Explain to them in detail why their choice could not be honored.

When the matches are decided and announced, distribute biographical sheets to give mentors and associates information about each other. Include photographs, professional information (e.g., schools, work experience, practice interests) and information about their personal lives (neighborhood, family, hobbies) that will make it easier for the relationship to get started.

A PROGRAM COORDINATOR

A program coordinator is essential to the success of a mentoring program. Others can be involved in matching, monitoring, and evaluating the program, but there should be one person who is accountable. If your firm has several offices, it is a good idea to have a firmwide program coordinator plus a local coordinator in each location or at least in your larger offices.

The program coordinator should have a thorough understanding and appreciation of mentoring and demonstrate the qualities of a good mentor. One of the main responsibilities of the program coordinator is to monitor the program to be sure that associates' needs are being met and the program's purpose is being achieved. Constant monitoring ensures that mentoring occurs, watches for and responds to early signs of problems, and facilitates continual improvement of the program. Because of the delicate political and interpersonal issues that can arise, the coordinator must have the trust and respect of all participants. The coordinator does not have to be a lawyer, but he or she must be someone who is respected by the lawyers in the program and supported by the leaders of the firm.

The responsibilities of the program coordinator will vary with the program objectives and the number of participants, and include:

- Acting as the liaison between the program participants and firm management;
- Managing program logistics;
- Preparing and overseeing the mentoring program budget;
- Organizing training programs;
- Helping match associates and mentors;
- Monitoring the progress of mentoring pairs;
- Informing participants of upcoming program events, mentoring resources, and opportunities;
- Reminding participants of their mentoring obligations;
- Responding to inquiries and offering advice about mentoring;
- Troubleshooting;
- Acting as a sounding board for program participants;
- Intervening when matches are not working well;

- Helping to resolve conflicts and problems that arise;

- Handling evaluation processes for the mentoring program and the mentoring relationships;

- Looking for opportunities to expand and improve the program; and

- Marketing the program internally.

Mentoring is only one of the activities that impact associates' professional development. Work assignments, the evaluation process, and skills training are all integral to associate development but may be separate from your mentoring program. The benefits of mentoring are enhanced when your mentoring program is coordinated with these other professional development functions. (See Chapter Nine.) The mentoring program coordinator should work with others in the firm to ensure that these interrelated professional development functions are smoothly and efficiently synchronized.

TRAINING

One of the most common reasons that mentoring programs fail is that many lawyers do not have the skills and behaviors required to make mentoring relationships productive. Because they are smart and successful, people assume that lawyers know how to be effective mentors and protégés. But cognitive ability is not enough for successful mentoring. Lawyers must learn mentoring dynamics, skills, and behaviors. The most effective approach to this kind of training is through interactive workshops that provide ample time for lawyers to practice what they learn.

Designing a training curriculum. For some lawyers, mentoring is a natural process; they act as mentors and seek out mentors regularly and easily. Lawyers who have had mentors in the past have their own experience as a reference; for them mentoring is a known process. For many lawyers, however, mentoring is neither natural nor familiar. If those lawyers are to be in successful mentoring relationships, they need to be prepared to assume their roles. They need to know what to do and how to do it.

To carry out their obligations, mentors need to know how to: listen effectively and advise constructively; identify associates' developmental needs and be sensitive to their professional anxieties; reduce associates' resistance to coaching and take advantage of receptive moments; and teach by asking questions rather than giving answers. They need to understand how to encourage associates to stretch beyond their comfort zone, how to be an effective advocate for their associates, and when to let associates fight their own battles.

For their part, associates have to listen effectively and be receptive to constructive advice. They have to learn not to take everything personally. They need to set their own development goals, be persistent in achieving those goals, and be appreciative of the mentor's help along the way. Most important, associates need to do excellent legal work and maintain a positive attitude so that the mentor wants to work with them.

A core training curriculum conveys the importance, nature, and interpersonal dynamics of the mentoring process; teaches the skills

---

TABLE 6. CORE TRAINING CURRICULUM

1. Mentoring dynamics[1]

- why mentoring is important
- how the mentoring process works
- commencing the relationship
- building trust
- building confidence
- support for risk-taking
- dealing with conflict
- transitions within the mentoring relationship
- ending the mentoring relationship

2. Mentoring skills

- attentive listening
- communication styles and differences
- learning styles and differences
- modeling
- counseling
- coaching

- setting development goals
- negotiating development plans
- delegation
- supervision
- feedback
- objective performance evaluations
- advocacy

3. Mentoring attitudes and behaviors

- self-awareness
- empathy
- dealing with differences[2]
- setting reasonable expectations
- taking initiative
- persistence
- demonstrating commitment
- being a worthy participant
- reflection
- showing appreciation

---

[1] For group mentoring, mentors need to also understand group dynamics and facilitation skills.

[2] Generational, gender, racial, ethnic, sexual orientation, disabilities.

that mentors and associates need to make mentoring work; and raises awareness of the attitudes and behaviors that contribute to successful mentoring. (See *Table 6*.)

Training that covers these topics will give participants the tools they need to accomplish the purpose of the mentoring relationship. The size and resources of your firm will dictate the scope of your training program. Although this list of curriculum elements may look daunting, most of these topics can be presented without an elaborate program and in a relatively short time. The training can be done by lawyers and managers in your firm if they have adequate training skills and the time and interest to do it. Alternatively, you can use an outside consultant or trainer to teach the curriculum or individual pieces of it. Whoever does the training must be sensitive to the intensely personal nature of many of these subjects and to the fears that prevent people from fully engaging in the learning process. Associates may be reluctant to say things that are critical of partners; partners may not want to reveal their own weaknesses; and both may be reluctant to voice unpopular feelings and beliefs they hold. Special measures should be taken to make people feel safe if they speak honestly.

Training should begin with an orientation when individuals start their mentoring relationships. Most formal mentoring programs match many mentoring pairs at once, e.g., after all new associates arrive. If that is the case, all mentoring pairs should attend a joint orientation session as part of the program's kick-off event. The orientation should cover, at a minimum, the dynamics of mentoring, the guidelines for mentoring in your program, and the roles and responsibilities of all participants. These areas can be covered in an hour or two depending on the scope and objectives of your program. Provide ample time for questions and answers, small group discussions, and interaction between mentors and associates. The orientation is also the time for firm leadership to emphasize the high priority that the firm places on mentoring and the firm's commitment to associate development through mentoring.

Training to teach skills and deal with attitudes will take place after your orientation, either within the mentoring context, or as part of a more global management skills training program. Because training sessions in these areas are intended to introduce new behaviors and change others, they require more time than is usually available at an orientation. These training sessions can be held all at once or over a period of time.

Although doing the training all at once may be more convenient, this kind of training works best if you give people a chance to process and practice what they learn in one area before moving on to another. One way to do this is with a series of lunchtime workshops over a period of weeks or even months. Ideally, each workshop should be interactive and cover no more than one or two topics in depth.

To supplement your firm's orientation and workshop sessions, you can provide personal coaching and group sessions. People who are having problems with a mentoring relationship may benefit from individual coaching, and coaching may also help mentor-associate pairs work through particular mentoring problems they are having. Group sessions where mentors, associates, or a combined group can discuss their mentoring experiences enable participants to learn more about the mentoring process and gain insights into their own mentoring relationships.

If diversity is a concern of your program, diversity training should also be included in your curriculum. This training should raise the awareness of all program participants regarding diversity issues and give them the skills to manage those issues. Mentors in particular should be shown how to establish trust and build confidence. Because of the influential role they play, mentors need to be comfortable and adept at working with people who are different.

Training in core curriculum topics should be provided for both mentors and associates. Some of these training sessions are more suitable for mentors alone and some for associates alone. Mentors need to know how to formulate and deliver advice about career paths, while associates need to know how to set development goals and ask for help and feedback. However, most training related to mentoring is best accomplished by having mentors and associates meet together. In the San Francisco office of Morrison & Foerster, for example, training is used to enhance an informal mentoring program. Although some workshops are designed primarily for mentors and others for associates, all attorneys are invited to attend all sessions.

One special advantage of this joint training is that everyone hears the same message, which clarifies program expectations and reduces misunderstanding. Joint sessions are especially helpful to define the kinds of behaviors acceptable within the mentoring context. For example, new associates are often reluctant to "bother" their mentors because they worry that the mentor will be annoyed, too busy, or think that the associate is being too pushy. In fact, mentors often do react that way. By learning about the mentoring process together, mentors come to understand that associates are expected to initiate and nudge their mentors when they need mentoring help, and associates learn how far they can go in doing so. Including associates and mentors in joint learning sessions also encourages mentored associates to start thinking like mentors themselves. By participating in interactive exercises that explain how to give constructive feedback or build trust, associates begin to appreciate what is involved in being a mentor and how they can become mentors to their peers and colleagues. This fosters a firm culture where mentoring is respected, ongoing, and natural.

ONGOING SUPPORT AND PROGRAM MONITORING

A structured mentoring program requires ongoing support. Getting a program up and running is only the beginning. In the most common scenario, mentoring receives a lot of attention when the program starts, but attention then dwindles over time. It is important for a firm to maintain the program's momentum from the outset by keeping participants engaged, informed, and enthusiastic. Some ideas for keeping the ball rolling are:

- Educational seminars and training programs;
- Tips for mentors and associates;
- Discussion groups for mentoring participants;
- Offsite retreats for mentoring participants;
- Educational articles about mentoring;
- An in-house mentoring newsletter;
- Periodic program updates; and
- Social events for mentors and their associates.

Communications about the program's status and progress will keep the program visible, stimulate participants to do what is expected of them, and entice non-participants to join the program in the next round. Through memos, emails, and newsletters, you can highlight mentoring events, spotlight lawyers in the program, and recount achievements of participants. You can also use these media to educate the firm about the dynamics of mentoring, effective mentoring techniques, and available training and resources for those interested in the mentoring program.

Written and electronic forms of communication are useful for conveying information, but personal interactions are more likely to spark excitement about the mentoring program. Holding group sessions gives participants a chance to share experiences, exchange ideas, and talk about what they are learning. Participants can describe techniques that worked for them and how they dealt with problems they may have faced. These groups may be limited to mentors or associates, or they may include both. Sessions can be structured (e.g., a presentation by a mentor, associate, or outside consultant on a relevant topic), or they can have an open agenda, leaving people free to raise any subject they wish to discuss. Either way, these sessions perform an important training and support function for the program.

Individual mentoring relationships also need to be monitored to ascertain whether mentoring relationships are working and program objectives are being met. This is the responsibility of the program coordinator and can be done either informally or through a formal reporting mechanism. Informally, the program coordinator can make inquiries about whether participants are satisfied with their relationship and how well they are doing in meeting the associate's developmental objectives. Alternatively, the program can build in a system that calls for periodic progress reports to be submitted to the program coordinator. The program coordinator can use this information to assess the quality of mentoring and make specific recommendations to enhance the mentoring experience.

EVALUATION

Ongoing monitoring helps the firm evaluate how well individual mentoring relationships are working. When formal mentoring relationships end, it is important to determine how well the relationships achieved their purpose. One way is to look at whether and to what extent the associates' developmental objectives were attained. For example, if an associate's objectives called for more client contact, success can be measured by the number and character of client interactions the associate had during the mentoring period.

It is also important to get feedback from program participants about the mentoring experience. Input should be solicited from both mentors and associates, either separately or together, using question-naires or interviews. Include questions that ask about satisfaction in general and very specific questions about the mentoring relationship (e.g., how often did you meet? who set the agenda for your meetings? was your mentor receptive to your questions? was the associate receptive to your advice? how did your mentor help you achieve your developmental goals?). Among other things, eliciting this information will help you:

■ Spot recurring mentoring issues or dilemmas;

■ Find flaws in your program design or matching process;

■ Suggest areas where further training or support may be needed;

■ Identify individual lawyers who are exceptional or problematic;

■ Identify excellent mentors who should be recognized and rewarded;

■ Identify mentors whose conduct is below the firm's expected standard;

■ Identify associates with leadership potential; and

■ Identify associates with remedial needs.

Keep in mind that associates may be reluctant to say bad things about a partner-mentor for fear of repercussions. Assurances of confidentiality may assuage their concerns and draw out useful information. When confidentiality is maintained as promised and associates see the evaluation process result in positive changes, their trust and support will grow.

In addition to evaluating mentoring relationships, the firm should evaluate the overall mentoring program. Program evaluation takes on a more global view to determine whether the program goals and objectives are being achieved and to find areas for improvement. Evaluations done in a regular and systematic way will enable the firm to identify the program's strengths and limitations, make adjustments based on what is learned, and determine whether the program is accomplishing its purpose. That is why it is so important to set clear, definite, and measurable goals when the program begins: evaluations can then assess how well those goals have been achieved. If, for example, a purpose of your mentoring program is to reduce associate turnover, the firm can track attrition rates, comparing figures from year to year, and see whether the program is having its intended impact.

Decide at the outset how — and how often — you will measure the program's success. Different types of data can be gathered at various stages of the program, and an in-depth evaluation should be conducted every year or two. Both quantitative and qualitative data are useful and can be gathered through informal feedback, surveys, interviews, and meetings. Some data-gathering approaches include:

- Soliciting informal feedback through an occasional email or phone call asking "How's it going?";

- Using interviews or surveys to assess the quality of participants' mentoring experience;

- Collecting suggestions and ideas that people submit on how to improve the program;

- Holding group meetings or an off-site retreat for participants to generate recommendations for program improvement; and

- A year or two after a formal mentoring relationship ends, asking associates whether and how the mentoring experience contributed to their professional development.

WRITTEN GUIDELINES

Mentoring programs need written guidelines to explain what is expected of participants and to minimize the chances for confusion or failure. Guidelines should clearly inform mentors and associates about their responsibilities in the mentoring program. They need not be exhaustive but they should be sufficiently detailed to provide clear guidance to program participants. The degree of detail will vary depending upon the complexity of your program. If your program is intended to make summer associates feel welcome in the firm, the guidelines will be brief and highlight the mentor's role in planning and involving the summer associate in social events. If, however, your program is designed to help mid-level associates do long-term career planning, then the guidelines will necessarily be more extensive.

At a minimum, your written guidelines should address the following points:

- Program purpose and objectives;

- How the program objectives should be met;

- How program objectives will be monitored;

- How the program will be evaluated;

- Responsibilities of the mentor;

- Responsibilities of the associate;

- How the mentoring relationship works;

- Role of the program coordinator;

- What to do if problems arise in the mentoring relationship;

- How mentors and associates will be matched;

- Duration of the mentoring relationship;

- Time commitment;

- How mentoring activities should be recorded on time sheets;

- Confidentiality; and

- Budget.

A summary of your guidelines should be distributed to all attorneys in the firm, not just those who are participating in the program. Everyone should appreciate and understand that this is a firm effort, not an isolated activity, and that the firm values mentoring highly. You want all lawyers to know what mentoring program participants are doing and to sensitize non-participants to the rigor of the mentoring enterprise. Distributing guidelines will help you encourage non-participating lawyers to join the program and, at a minimum, to intensify their informal mentoring activities.

INCENTIVES FOR MENTORING

If you want mentoring to happen, honor and reward it. Don't just pay it lip service. Let everyone see that the firm really values good mentors with tangible recognition and appropriate compensation. Most firms do this for rainmakers and lawyers who bill high hours, but if mentoring is truly a firm priority, it should be treated the same way. Otherwise, the firm's reward systems may actually discourage people from mentoring.

To illustrate this point, take Rob's situation. Rob is a senior litigation partner in a firm well known for its associate training program. For many years Rob has been the partner in charge of associate training.

He enjoys teaching and is considered one of the firm's best mentors. The associates love to work with him and his partners respect both his legal ability and the strong bonds he forms with the associates. None of the associates who have worked with Rob in the last three years have left the firm. Rob logged a total of 2300 hours last year, of which 500 hours were spent in non-billable mentoring and training activities, and 100 hours were non-billable work on the hiring committee. During his year-end interview with the compensation committee, the committee told him that his mentoring efforts were commendable "but they aren't bringing in any cash," and, since he only billed 1700 hours, the firm will have to reduce his overall compensation. The committee also told him to "get those billable hours up."

Because the committee focused on revenues, they failed to appreciate the substantial amount of money Rob has saved the firm by retaining valuable associates. For each associate who leaves a firm, the replacement costs are about two times the associate's salary. In today's market, this comes to hundreds of thousands of dollars. By developing and retaining associates and avoiding those replacement costs, Rob's work as a mentor may in fact have been more profitable for the firm than the hours other partners spent in billable work or business development.

Unless mentoring is rewarded, good mentors like Rob find themselves with less money and influence than their colleagues. Because of the primacy of billable work, attorneys who would be excellent mentors decline mentoring opportunities. Associates likewise get the message that they should not spend time in activities that are not billable, and they hesitate to approach potential mentors because they think it would be an imposition on them. Consequently, they do not seek the help and advice that they need. This reduces the frequency and quality of mentoring, which in turn delays associate development and leads to higher associate turnover.

To make it clear that mentoring is not only valued but expected, a firm should encourage and reward lawyers for mentoring activities. Here are a few ideas:

- Give special credit for time spent in mentoring activities;

- Award compensation bonuses for lawyers identified as good mentors;

■ Award bonuses tied to associate retention (e.g., for lawyers who have low turnover rates among the associates they mentor);

■ Set up a "mentoring account" which allocates a certain number of hours to mentoring activities;

■ Give recognition awards to outstanding mentors (e.g, best mentor of the year, month, department); and

■ Acknowledge lawyers by name for "best mentoring practices."

CHAPTER 7

PROGRAM PARTICIPATION

"[P]ower in organizations is the capacity
generated by relationships."

MARGARET J. WHEATLEY

MENTORS

■ CHARACTERISTICS OF GOOD LAW FIRM MENTORS

Mentors come in all styles, shapes, and temperaments. There is no "standard" model. They may be patient advisers who encourage you to move toward a goal or demanding taskmasters who present you with difficult challenges. Mentors may be calm listeners who gently draw out your latent talents or gruff directors who aggressively push you to ever higher levels of performance. Their approaches may vary but what they all have in common is a willingness to invest time and energy helping less experienced lawyers realize their highest potential. Most mentoring skills can be taught and someone with the desire to be a mentor can learn those skills, but the most effective mentors share a common underlying mindset: they care about the people they mentor and are generous with their time and wisdom.

Good mentors have many characteristics that should be considered in selecting mentors for your program. Of the attributes on the following list, the first four are mandatory; the others are desirable but optional. All mentors should possess some of them; few mentors will have them all.

Characteristics of Good Mentors:

- Interest in helping associates learn and grow professionally;

- Willingness to share professional experience and knowledge;

- Expertise that will help achieve the program objectives;

- Accessibility;

- Empathy;

- Credibility;

- Confidence that they can offer something of value;

- A favorable reputation in the firm, especially among those to be mentored;

- Excellent interpersonal skills;

- Exemplary lawyering skills;

- Good delegation and supervision skills;

- Strong coaching and counseling skills;

- Ability to be both challenging and supportive

- Good communication skills (listening as well as speaking)

- Ability to relate to junior associates;

- Willingness to learn from associates;

- Interest in being a role model; and

- Patience.

To this list of mentor attributes we might also add "power and influence in the firm," "prominence in the community," and "a strong client base." For a new or junior associate, these characteristics may be desirable, but they are not essential. However, they are of critical importance for junior partners and senior associates for whom having an influential champion and sponsor can be instrumental for career advancement.

One time when it is important to have prominent partners serve as mentors is when you are implementing your mentoring program for the first time. Having these partners involved will signal the firm's commitment to mentoring, give your program more credibility, and help recruit other lawyers to participate as mentors.

■ RECRUITING MENTORS

Mentoring programs depend on the talent and dedication of mentors. To have a viable program, you must nurture the excellent mentors you have and recruit others who have the potential and interest. In choosing mentors, consider the impact they will have on their assigned associates as role models, teachers, and counselors. Look for the behaviors, attitudes, and work styles the firm would like to perpetuate. Every firm has a few lawyers who are natural mentors and with whom associates love to work. Usually, there are too few of these mentors to go around and only a handful of associates reap the benefits of their mentorship.

Mentors need not be all things to all associates. Instead, they should concentrate on doing what they do best. Rather than looking for a superstar mentor, associates should take advantage of a mentor's special talents. Many lawyers who lack some desirable mentoring attributes have other skills and traits that are of tremendous value. Every lawyer has something of value to offer as a mentor. A bombastic litigator may have no patience for teaching trial advocacy but may love to bring associates along to court and debrief them afterward. A senior partner who is extremely shy in social settings may be superb at building an associate's self-confidence in a one-on-one relationship.

Similarly, don't assume that you know who the good mentors are. Just because someone is charismatic or powerful does not mean they will be a good mentor. Firms are often surprised at who their good and bad mentors are. Karen, a mentoring program coordinator in a San Francisco firm, was surprised when associates gave terrible reviews to a prominent trial lawyer who for years had been known as a terrific mentor. For unclear reasons, his attitude toward associates had changed. They complained that he was sarcastic, became surly when they asked questions, and often humiliated them. On the other hand, associates gave high marks to a very quiet, unassuming partner with a very low profile whom they regarded as a dedicated teacher and adviser.

■ DETERMINING WHO THE MENTORS IN YOUR PROGRAM WILL BE

The potential mentors in your program include partners, associates, retired partners, counsel,[1] and non-lawyer office personnel. Associates would prefer to have partners — especially powerful and influential partners — as their mentors. After all, these are the people who will have the greatest impact on associates' careers. But using partners as mentors in your program may not be in the associates' or the firm's best interests. When deciding who should be mentors, your first question should be: Which potential mentors will best suit our program objectives? If your program is intended to focus on career planning and advancement, perhaps all mentors should be partners — and influential partners at that. But if the program's primary purpose is to introduce new associates around the office, these partners may be wasted in the mentoring role. It may be wiser to have mentors who are closer in age or experience to the associates. New associates are more apt to go to another associate for basic practice information than to approach a senior partner even if the partner is their assigned mentor. If your firm feels it is important for associates to interact with prominent partners, one way to do that is through group mentoring. (See Chapter Ten.) Group mentoring satisfies the associates' desire to get to know these partners and exposes the partners to several associates without as significant a time commitment as one-on-one mentoring.

Likewise, do not assume that mentors must always be older than the lawyers they mentor. In areas involving technology, for example, many young lawyers have far more experience and knowledge than the older lawyers in your firm, and a technology-savvy associate may be a helpful mentor to a senior lawyer. This kind of "reverse" mentoring has been used at Procter & Gamble since the early 1990s. In response to a continued loss of women managers, Procter & Gamble started a "Mentor Up" program in which junior women are paired with senior male managers. In a reversal of the traditional mentoring model, these junior women act as mentors who provide senior managers with

---

1 Many firms now have lawyers who are "of counsel," "senior counsel," "special counsel," or some other variation of this term. These are usually experienced lawyers who are formally affiliated with the firm but are neither partners nor associates. The term "counsel" is used here as a catch-all for lawyers in those positions.

informal feedback about how to manage issues specific to women. In the first two years of this program, the company was able to reduce its loss of women managers by 25 percent.

Other potential mentors are retired partners and counsel. Many of these lawyers enjoy teaching and would welcome an opportunity to work with associates. Provided that they can relate well to young associates, retired partners and counsel can be valuable mentors who can share years of accumulated wisdom as well as offer guidance on specific practice skills. This has worked very well for two San Francisco firms, 280–lawyer McCutchen, Doyle, Brown & Enersen, and 70-lawyer Severson & Werson. At each of these firms, a retired litigation partner serves as a mentor to litigation associates and monitors their training, skills development, and work experience.

A valuable source of mentors that law firms often overlook is non-lawyer personnel. Executive directors and other key administrators and managers have a great deal to offer attorneys, especially attorneys who are new partners or approaching partnership. If your mentoring program is designed for leadership development, if you hope to groom future managing partners and practice group leaders, or if you want to give lawyers a better understanding of business and management, these individuals have the skills and knowledge to make a valuable contribution as mentors.

ASSOCIATES

■ ASSOCIATE CHARACTERISTICS CONDUCIVE TO MENTORING

In order to make the most of a mentoring program, associates need to be open to the mentoring process and committed to the success of the mentoring program. Like their counterpart mentors, some associates will find the mentoring relationship natural and easy. Others may feel awkward or threatened. Your orientation and training programs should acknowledge these differences and help make everyone comfortable with the mentoring process.

The mentoring relationship will be most effective when the associate defines his or her needs, issues, and problems. The mentor's coaching and advice can then be directed where the associate will find it most valuable. Some of the characteristics and attitudes that will help associates make the most of the mentoring relationship include:

- Being committed to excellence in their work;

- Understanding their responsibility for their own career development;

- Thinking about their ambitions and career goals;

- Taking initiative and following through on mentoring activities;

- Being willing to speak up and to ask questions of their mentors;

- Being eager to take on challenging new responsibilities;

- Observing carefully;

- Being receptive to feedback and coaching;

- Being open to receiving help; and

- Reflecting on and learning from their mistakes.

■ DETERMINING WHO WILL BE MENTORED IN YOUR PROGRAM

The objectives of your mentoring program will expressly prescribe the lawyers who will be mentored. Corporations sometimes select only key employees for formal mentoring programs (e.g., women, minorities, high-potential managers), but law firms rarely limit their programs this way. Law firms are loathe to exclude individuals on the basis of personal characteristics or perceived ability because every associate should be someone with "high potential." Instead, firms group lawyers into certain categories based on practice areas (e.g., entertainment lawyers), experience level (e.g., first-year associates), or status (e.g., lateral partners). Rather than select only a few individuals, law firm programs commonly include all associates in the designated group. For example, if a firm's objective is to improve the management skills of mid-level associates, the targeted lawyers would be all mid-level associates with responsibility for managing others. If the objective is to acculturate lateral associates into the firm, the targeted lawyers would be all lateral associates.

Some law firms are beginning to promote lawyers to interim positions between associate and partnership status, and to tailor mentoring programs to certain individuals based upon their ability and future prospects. If your firm decides to limit assigned mentors to particular individuals, be sure that the criteria for selection and the reasons for exclusion are very clearly explained; that they do not stigmatize the individuals selected or discriminate against those who are not; and that they are applied fairly. If participation is perceived negatively, or if the criteria are believed to be inequitable, you will do more harm than good for program participants and the firm.

One group of lawyers who should not be overlooked in your mentoring program is associates who work part-time. Increasingly, lawyers are working reduced schedules. It is a good idea to include part-time lawyers in your program if they are willing to participate and their schedules can be accommodated. If they are talented lawyers whom the firm hopes to keep, they should be invited to participate in the program. Offering to include them shows these lawyers that the firm values their contributions and supports their continued professional development. If you decide to make mentors available to part-time lawyers, respect their part-time schedules and ensure that their participation is voluntary. Some part-time lawyers are paid only for billable work. If this is the case in your firm, then the firm has to decide whether part-time lawyers will be compensated beyond their billable hours for time spent in the mentoring program. From a long-term perspective, compensating part-time associates for non-billable mentoring activities may well be worth the investment.

MENTOR–ASSOCIATE WORK RELATIONSHIP ISSUES

■ CLEARLY DEFINED ROLES AND RESPONSIBILITIES

Lawyers who are asked to take part in mentoring relationships need to have their responsibilities explained to them. One of the reasons mentoring programs fail is that participants do not know what they are supposed to do. You cannot assume that either mentors or associates know what is expected of them. In order to be sure that the objectives of your program will be carried out, you must define in detail what their roles and responsibilities will be. This information should be presented at the beginning of the mentoring program during orientation, covered in training sessions and ongoing support efforts, and documented in written guidelines. Writing it down prevents confusion and facilitates compliance by helping lawyers understand what they must do to achieve the program's purpose.

If roles and responsibilities are not clarified, mentors' and associates' views of the mentoring process may conflict with your program objectives. Let's say that your program is intended to make the associate responsible for setting up meetings with the mentor on a regular basis. This contrasts with traditional mentoring relationships in which mentors take the lead in initiating meetings. Unless the new and different ground rules of your program are explained to both mentors and associates, they may start off on the wrong foot or not get started at all. Associates may be too intimidated to approach partners or may believe they should wait to be called, and mentors may assume that they are the ones who control the mentoring agenda. Although this may seem like a trivial point, a clear understanding of who is supposed to take the lead will ensure that the pair approach the mentoring process in harmony.

Clarification also avoids the disappointment that may be caused by incorrect expectations. Associates want "mentoring," but they are not sure what mentoring entails or how to get it. They may assume that the mentor is someone to go to with every kind of question, personal as well as professional; that they and their mentor will become close friends; that the mentor will shepherd their career for a lifetime; or that having a mentor is a promise of advancement. Depending upon the program's purpose, any of those assumptions might be right or wrong.

Similarly, partners have to be told what it means to be a mentor in your program. Partners who have had mentors themselves have some idea of what mentoring looks like, at least from their own experience, but they may not have a clue about what they should be doing for an associate in your firm's program. They need to understand not just what the program objectives are, but how they can carry them out. Even for the most simple program objective, mentors need guidance. For example, mentors are often told they should make the associate "feel at home," but what does that mean? Is one lunch enough? Should they invite the associate to their home for dinner? Should they introduce the associate to the people on his or her floor? On all floors? You do not have to list every activity in exhaustive detail, but some guidance and specificity will eliminate much of the guesswork and make it more likely that your program objectives will be met.

The need for guidance is even greater when the mentor is expected to help the associate address a developmental need (e.g., work more independently, improve negotiation skills, become more assertive). To do this, mentors have to work with the associate to identify the associate's needs and negotiate a mutually agreeable development plan. Associates must play an active role in this process but busy partners often do not have the patience or skill to go through all the necessary steps. Instead, they prefer to solve the associate's problem themselves or to decide and impose their own development plan on the associate. This will frustrate the associate's effort to take responsibility for his or her own development and will undermine the whole point of your program.

■ CONFIDENTIALITY

Mentoring involves a certain degree of risk. In the course of a mentoring relationship, associates — and sometimes mentors — disclose needs, fears, and problems that make them vulnerable. One may learn that the other has a problem which is not generally known but may place the individual and the firm in jeopardy (e.g., an ethical breach, depression, alcoholism). Certain issues may be discussed that create personal or professional complications for one of the mentoring pair, such as an associate informing the mentor that the associate is interviewing for a job at another firm or is romantically involved with a partner.

It is important for the integrity of the mentoring relationship that the question of confidentiality be decided at the outset. Some lawyers are open to discussing confidential or sensitive issues, while others are adamantly opposed; many will feel uncomfortable even bringing up the subject of confidentiality for fear of inviting an embarrassing or troubling dialogue. Your firm can issue a confidentiality policy or it can leave the decision up to the lawyers in each mentoring pair. A policy about confidentiality might provide that all communications are confidential or that all communications are not confidential. If the policy favors confidentiality, mentors and associates are expected to keep communications between them strictly confidential. The firm should make it clear whether the policy is absolute or whether it is subject to exceptions. Two common exceptions are that (1) the mentoring pair can override the policy by mutual agreement, or (2) confidentiality will be presumed except where disclosure is required by law, the rules of professional responsibility, or another firm policy. If disclosure of a confidential communication is required, the affected party should be notified in advance, and the disclosure should be limited to those who need to know. If the firm's policy states that communications between mentor and associate will not be treated as confidential, then an exception should be allowed for parties who want to discuss issues confidentially. The opportunity for one party to confide in the other is integral to any mentoring relationship. While the firm may wish to make lawyers aware that confidentiality is not part of its official mentoring policy, mentors and associates should be permitted to discuss sensitive subjects without fear of exposure.

In any case, mentors and associates should be instructed to be cautious before raising issues they wish to keep private. If there is any doubt in their minds about whether a subject they wish to discuss will be kept confidential, they should ask before making any disclosures and confirm that the matter will remain private between them. They should also be instructed that there are some subjects that cannot remain confidential, even if both parties want it otherwise. Most notably, if the mentor is a partner and the associate tells him or her of sexual improprieties by another partner or a client, the mentor is legally obligated to report the possible sexual harassment.

■ WHEN RELATIONSHIP PROBLEMS ARISE

When you assign lawyers to a mentoring relationship, some of the matches will be less than ideal. Lawyers may find they do not like each other, or their personalities and styles may clash, making it difficult to work together. Mentors may become overly controlling, telling the associate precisely what to do and how to do it, or unresponsive and remote, refusing to spend any time with the associate. When these situations occur, associates often feel trapped and frustrated, but they may be reluctant or afraid to complain. Likewise, some associates may be problematic for their mentors. They may fail to follow through on commitments, demand too much of the mentor, or have a negative attitude or a chip on their shoulder.

When relationship problems occur, quick intervention is necessary. A watchful program coordinator will find the source of the problem and determine whether the relationship can be salvaged. The program coordinator can work with the pair or bring in someone else to help the mentor and associate resolve the problem. Sometimes a busy lawyer simply forgot to do what was promised or had misguided expectations. A reminder or suggestion by the program coordinator may be all that is needed to get the mentoring pair back on track. Other times, the problems are more fundamental and cannot be remedied. If the problem is incurable, the relationship should be severed. Unless lawyers in bad relationships are reassigned, they may remain frustrated and unfulfilled, and the benefits of your mentoring program will be lost to them. Subsequent mentoring assignments for these lawyers should take this experience into account so that similar mistakes are not repeated.

■ SPECIAL CONSIDERATIONS WHEN MENTORS AND ASSOCIATES WORK TOGETHER

Law firms often have a hard time deciding whether the mentor and associate should work together on client matters. One school of thought argues that associates will be more comfortable in relationships with mentors who do not supervise their work. The other school contends that mentoring relationships are stronger and more successful when the associate and mentor work together. Formal mentoring programs can succeed with either approach, but the latter provides a context for a more natural and sustained mentoring relationship. In either case, tradeoffs have to be made, and the firm has to decide which approach will better accomplish its program objectives.

The most substantial benefit when mentors and associates do not work together is increased candor. Associates may open up more easily to mentors who will not be supervising their work, giving them performance reviews, or making decisions about their assignments and advancement. Associates want to have a mentor they can confide in about professional fears, doubts, or insecurities. Associates will feel freer to talk about these concerns with a mentor who has no immediate control over their work assignments or promotion.

When mentors and associates work together, there is a tension between the mentor's roles as supervisor and as confidante. Associates worry that confiding in a mentor who is also a work supervisor might have negative repercussions: poor work assignments, bad evaluations, stigmatization, or even loss of partnership opportunities. Meryl's situation illustrates the dilemma. Meryl is a real estate associate in a mid-size firm. Her assigned mentor, Brian, is in the same department. They had a good relationship at first, and Meryl felt comfortable talking with Brian about many issues — so long as they did not involve work she was doing for his clients. When Meryl brought up matters unrelated to Brian's clients, he was understanding and supportive, but if Meryl mentioned problems about the work she was doing for Brian's clients, Brian became critical and judgmental. Eventually, she hesitated to confide in Brian at all.

On the other hand, few associates will disclose their fears and anxieties to someone simply because that person has been designated their mentor. Associates are appropriately suspicious and reluctant to share confidences with anyone who may have an impact on their jobs. The basis of any mentoring relationship is trust, which cannot be assigned or imposed; it must be earned. It develops over time as people get to know each other. As a practical matter, trust will take longer to develop when the mentor and associate do not work together. It is actually more likely to happen when a mentor and associate come into regular contact during the course of work.

Working together guarantees that the mentor and associate have a natural and ongoing reason to interact. When they share common client interests and have regular contact, trust is more likely to take root. Trust develops when there is a shared sense of competence and respect. When the mentor and associate work together, the associate finds it easier to approach the mentor to talk or seek advice, and has more opportunities to observe the mentor as a role model. The mentor also has an easier time observing the associate at work, judging the associate's professional ability and maturity, and identifying areas for potential growth.

In addition, mentors are more inclined to pay attention to lawyers working on their cases. In that situation, mentoring seems less of a time burden for the mentor; the mentor has an incentive to do in-depth analysis of the associate's work; and the mentoring process assumes greater relevance and meaning. Because they have an ongoing work relationship, mentoring sessions can be a natural outgrowth of the work relationship. As a result, even though mentor and associate are assigned to each other, their relationship will feel more spontaneous and informal. As an added benefit, mentoring in the regular course of client work is often billable.

Likewise, if your firm is organized into practice groups, it is best if your mentors and associates are in the same group. Associates need to build strong ties where they do their legal work. There are some exceptions when it is important for associates to work with lawyers in other practice groups. (In corporate programs, cross-department matching is common. See Chapter Eleven.) For example, if senior associates need exposure to other practices and partners in order to be considered for partnership, they might be matched with mentors in groups other than their own. If a practice group is so small that it does not have enough mentors, try to combine two or more practice groups (e.g., land use planning and environmental law) where clients overlap and lawyers frequently work together.

■ How the Mentor Relates to the Associate's Supervising Attorneys

Every firm has its own approach to associate work assignments. Whether or not the mentor and associate work together, your program guidelines should clarify if and how the mentor will be involved in the work assignment process. Ideally, if your mentoring program objectives deal with professional development (as opposed to orientation), your assignment process will be coordinated with your mentoring program. In that way, an associate's experience and workload can be tailored to promote the associate's development. Whether or not the mentor is also a supervisor, the program guidelines should clarify how the mentor should relate to the partners who supervise the associate's work.

A mentor who is also a supervisor may pose some special issues. Without clarifying guidelines, some mentors who have associates assigned to them may become overly possessive of their associates' time. They may insist that the associate give all the mentor's work priority or refuse to let the associate work with other partners. This puts the associate in a difficult position and generates resentment among the mentor's partners. This ill will may place the entire mentoring program in jeopardy.

Your firm should also address other aspects of the mentor's relationship to the associate's supervising attorneys:

- Will the mentor mediate between partners who are making conflicting demands on the associate?

- Should the mentor keep other supervising lawyers informed of the associate's mentoring activities?

- How will the mentor determine if the associate's work with other attorneys is helping to accomplish the associate's developmental objectives?

- What authority does the mentor have if the associate is not getting the experience needed to accomplish the associate's developmental objectives?

■ THE MENTOR'S ROLE IN ASSOCIATE EVALUATIONS

Mentors can be instrumental in associates' annual and semi-annual performance reviews. Too often, performance reviews are cursory and perfunctory, and opportunities for coaching are overlooked. Reviews should be used to help associates understand the areas in which they are doing well or need improvement, but more importantly, they are a time to assess developmental progress and set goals for further development. Either through direct participation during the review itself, or by counseling the associate before or after the review, the mentor can make the review more constructive and meaningful.

Mentors should receive copies of the associate's written evaluations, either in their entirety or in summary before the associate is reviewed in person. If mentors meet with the associates in advance, they can help them interpret the contents and nuances of the evaluations. They can use the evaluations to counsel and coach associates on how to conduct themselves in the review. A well-prepared associate is better able to listen and address key points in the review meeting, and the review itself is less emotional and more productive. If mentors do not review the evaluations with associates prior to the review, they still can debrief the associate afterward. Because associates are anxious during the review, they may not fully understand and appreciate what they are told. Mentors can go over the associates' evaluations and help the associates make sense of what they were told.

As a coach, mentors perform a very practical function — they help the associate translate the feedback from the review into concrete steps for improvement. During most associate reviews, partners tell associates where they need improvement, but they rarely help associates plan how to make the necessary changes. Mentors can turn feedback into action. They can work with associates to set new performance goals and determine how and when those goals will be achieved. By setting specific goals, a plan, and a timetable, the associate and mentor can measure the associate's future progress.

If the associate and the mentor have a good relationship, the mentor might attend the associate's performance review meeting. The mentor's presence may help alleviate some of the associate's anxiety, ensure that the associate clearly understands the significance of what the partners' evaluations mean, and help the associate begin the process of setting new developmental goals. Mentors sometimes feel anxious themselves about giving associates bad news in an evaluation, and many mentors worry that doing so may interfere with their developmental role. But part of a mentor's responsibility is to give honest feedback to the associate so that the associate can develop effective strategies for improvement, or, if necessary, assess other job or career options.

Associates usually presume that having a mentor participate in the evaluation process will work in their favor, but that is not always the result. Associates need to understand that the mentor may not be their best friend. If an associate does legal work directly for a mentor, the mentor will submit an evaluation of the associate's performance and potential. When mentors share their assessments of associates with the partnership, they can have a powerful impact on the associate's reputation, standing, and prospects in the firm. A mentor who looks favorably on an associate can be a great advocate for that associate. However, if the mentor feels that the associate lacks what it takes to succeed in the firm, a negative evaluation can be devastating.

A thorny issue may arise in the evaluation process when the mentor has sensitive or confidential knowledge about the associate. (See the comments on confidentiality under "Mentor–Associate Work Relationship Issues" earlier in this chapter.) Some law firms recuse mentors from evaluating their assigned associates so that their communications can be kept confidential. This allows associates to be more candid about any work or self-esteem problems they face, while the mentor can be more frank and direct in coaching and advising the associate. However, mentors are an important source of information for the firm about the associate. There are times when the mentor has confidential information that may impact on the firm's decisions regarding hiring and staffing needs or on the promotion or even continued employment of the associate. Dilemmas may arise when the associate confides a significant personal failing, shows a serious lack in judgment, reveals plans to leave the firm, or exhibits behavior that is detrimental to the interests of the firm. The mentor may face conflicts between the pledge of confidentiality to the associate and the obligation to disclose such knowledge to the firm. The firm's policy must make clear at the outset of the mentoring program the extent of the mentor's obligations to the firm regarding information learned from the associate, and when, if ever, those obligations take precedence over the mentoring program's provisions regarding confidentiality. Associates and mentors both need to know when the mentor's obligations to the firm supersede any promise of confidentiality.

■ THE NUMBER OF MENTORS ASSIGNED TO AN ASSOCIATE

In large law firm mentoring programs, it may be desirable to have more than one mentor assigned to an associate. In a large organization, having two mentors increases the associate's internal network. While partners or senior lawyers act as mentors for guidance regarding assignments, performance, or career issues, a more junior lawyer may be assigned as a mentor for orientation purposes. A good example of this approach is seen at Orrick, Herrington & Sutcliffe, where each new associate is assigned to a non-partner mentor and a partner mentor. The non-partner mentor is assigned to the associate for the first six months after the associate arrives to welcome the associate into the firm and give advice about day-to-day issues. Partner mentors are formally assigned for one year, after which they are encouraged to continue as mentors informally. Both partner and non-partner mentors are expected to help integrate the associate into the firm during the early stages of employment, but the partner mentor is also expected to deal with the associate's performance, work experience, and developmental goals.

■ THE NUMBER OF ASSOCIATES ASSIGNED TO A MENTOR

Most law firms have fewer mentors than associates, and allocating these mentors to the associates who need their help may present a challenge. If you overload your mentors with too many associates, they will not be able to serve the associates adequately, their other work may suffer, and they may burn out. As a general rule, keep the ratio of associates to mentors as low as possible. Usually, it is advisable to limit each mentor to no more than one or two associates. The exact ratio depends on the degree of time and effort expected of the mentor. Where the mentor is expected to work closely with the associate for a year or more on developmental goals, more than one or two associates per mentor may be unreasonable. However, in an orientation-focused mentoring program, where there is little ongoing work and the relationship is short-term, a higher number of associates per mentor is acceptable. If you do not have enough mentors to keep the associate/mentor ratio low, consider using a group mentoring format instead. (See Chapter Ten.)

CHAPTER 8

Making the Case for a Mentoring Program in Your Firm

"Organizations are no longer built on force but on trust. . . . Taking responsibility for relationships is therefore an absolute necessity. It is a duty"

PETER F. DRUCKER

Determining Readiness

Before you decide to start a program, be sure the culture and work environment in your firm, as well as the lawyers, will support a mentoring program. Below are the questions you must answer.

1. What do you hope to achieve with a mentoring program?

If your firm is considering a mentoring program, the first step is to understand the firm's motivation for having one. You must carefully analyze the needs of the firm and of your attorneys, and determine whether and how a mentoring program will address those needs. The best motivation for a formal program is to be sure that all attorneys receive the attention, guidance, and training that they need to become proficient, capable, and successful lawyers. This reflects a proactive interest in associate development.

Some firms undertake a mentoring program as a response to negative trends or complaints. That's fine so long as a mentoring program is the right approach to the underlying problem. Mentoring is a useful strategy but not a panacea. If associates are leaving because your firm's technology is obsolete or its policies are inflexible, a mentoring program will not stop them from going. Too many law firms look to mentoring programs as a "cure" for unhappy, dissatisfied associates. They implement a mentoring program as a knee-jerk reaction to bad reviews from associates in *The American Lawyer* or some other legal publication. While mentoring may ameliorate the dissatisfaction of some lawyers, mentoring by itself is probably not enough to do the trick. Mentoring works best as one component of a comprehensive associate development effort that encompasses training, work assignments, and evaluation. (See Chapter Nine.)

2. Are the firm's leaders committed to a structured mentoring program?

Strong support from the firm's leaders is imperative; without it, your program will not succeed. More than simply endorsing a structured mentoring program, your leaders must persuade the firm to make the program happen. Most importantly, leaders should participate in the program as mentors and as role models for other mentors. They must recognize the value of time devoted to mentoring, and be willing to support lawyers who engage in mentoring. They must be willing to allocate the resources necessary to make the program work, such as time and money for training and administrative support. If you do not have key partners on board, your initial task is to convince them that mentoring should be a top firm priority.

3. What has been the firm's past experience with mentoring programs?

The firm's history in mentoring and professional development can provide useful lessons as you contemplate a mentoring program. If the firm had a mentoring program in the past, find out why it was discontinued. If it worked well before, talk to earlier participants, look through any old files that may exist, and try to learn from past successes. Build on earlier achievements. If relevant, incorporate practices from those earlier efforts in designing your new program. If earlier attempts at a mentoring program did not succeed, try to determine the reasons. Look for structural defects and points of resistance — e.g., whether the guidelines were ambiguous, lawyers refused to participate in certain types of activities, or key individuals or practice groups were uncooperative. You want to avoid making the same mistakes when you put your new program together. Of course, if the previous effort failed because the firm was not really committed to the program, then you need to determine whether there has been a sufficient change in attitude to make the program succeed this time around.

4. Will your firm's culture support a structured mentoring program?

Firm culture involves the beliefs and deeply held values of the organization. Each firm has its own unique culture with distinctive values, rituals, norms, attitudes, and beliefs that shape every aspect of firm life. The core values of a firm's culture determine how the firm functions, including its structure, strategy, management, and leadership. These core values impact the way people relate to each other in the work environment and in their attitudes toward mentoring and professional development. As Collins and Porras point out in *Built to Last: Successful Habits of Visionary Companies*, there is no one "right" set of core values. The crucial factor is not the content of a firm's beliefs but the depth of those beliefs and how consistently they are followed.

Mentoring requires a culture where people help each other. To fully embrace a mentoring program, your firm culture must value associate development and be receptive to an organized and systematic effort to promote it. You cannot successfully introduce a mentoring program into an environment that discourages interaction between associates and partners, inhibits lawyers from sharing knowledge, or condones the hoarding of information. If the firm's culture is so staunchly individualistic that lawyers resist cooperating in any organized effort, it is unlikely that they will accept a mentoring program. Likewise, if the attorneys are so egocentric that they believe associates are there only to serve them, no mentoring program will work. Mentoring programs can work in cultures that favor individualism and self-interest, but only when the culture places greater value on the professional development of its lawyers.

Within a large firm, there may be different and competing subcultures, and the firm may only be able to support mentoring in certain offices or practice groups. In the same firm, associates and partners may work together collaboratively and harmoniously in the secured transactions group, while the intellectual property group suffers from internal competition and dissension. A mentoring program will work in the former group and probably fail in the latter. If that is the case in your firm, it is advisable not to implement your mentoring program firmwide but to start your mentoring program in the group where success is most likely.

How can you tell if your firm culture will support a formal mentoring program? One way is to look at your current professional development efforts. If your firm has a thriving in-house training program, takes associate evaluations seriously, and has lawyers who enjoy working together, a mentoring program is a logical next step. If, however, your training is spotty, evaluations are irregular and perfunctory, and partners distrust each other, you have a lot of work to do before you can embark on a mentoring program. Firm culture develops over time; it cannot be changed merely by adopting a vision statement or declaring new values. If your firm culture is not currently conducive to mentoring, that does not mean you cannot have a mentoring program. It does mean, however, that you must make some fundamental changes before mentoring can become a widespread practice.

5. Will the current conditions in your firm sustain a mentoring program?

The health of the firm has a direct impact on mentoring. When there is a lot of work, formal mentoring is especially appealing to partners who want more help, have more reasons to delegate work, and have to get associates up to speed more quickly. Even when work is slow for a time, partners can use some of their free time to work more closely with associates in a mentoring program. Likewise, in times of rapid change, mentoring can ease the way. When a firm is growing, expanding, merging, or going through restructuring, mentoring facilitates the change process and builds bonds among lawyers. However, if a firm is in economic distress or organizational turmoil, partners will be too preoccupied with these problems to accept any new mentoring initiative, at least until the firm regains its health.

6. What support must be developed for your firm to initiate a mentoring program?

Surveys, focus groups, interviews, and open discussion sessions can tell you how the firm views mentoring and how easy or hard it will be to institute a formal program. Involving members of various constituent groups (e.g., associates and partners, men and women, minority attorneys, offices and practice groups) in this investigative process has several advantages. It elicits various constituents' interests and concerns that must be taken into account in designing the program and builds support for the program as you plan it. People who contribute to the design of the program have a stake in its outcome; they become supporters who will market the program and participate in it.

In addition, you can gauge the willingness of lawyers to take part in the program. A mentoring program depends on the active and voluntary participation of the firm's lawyers. It is important for mentors to be committed, not simply assigned. If you find that the rank and file are not willing to participate, you need to rethink your plans. You may have to market the program more effectively, change your objectives, or drop the idea completely.

In doing your investigation, be sure to include people who may question the need for a structured program. Their views will alert you to potential problem areas and help you plan how to overcome any resistance you may encounter. Winning over naysayers can add to the program's credibility and desirability.

Selling a Mentoring Program

■ Promoting Benefits

If you determine that your firm can and should support a formal mentoring program, you may still have to convince some members of the firm that such a program is a good idea. In making the case for a mentoring program, begin by citing the many benefits of mentoring elaborated in Chapter Three and the benefits of mentoring programs described in Chapter Seven. A formal mentoring program:

- Reduces attrition;

- Increases firm profitability;

- Promotes attorney training and development;

- Fosters leadership development;

- Provides widespread access to mentors;

- Ensures quality mentoring;

- Sets guidelines that manage expectations;

- Identifies associate problems early;

- Enhances communication within the firm;

- Manifests the firm's commitment to attorney development; and

- Makes informal mentoring more likely to happen.

■ REBUTTING OBJECTIONS

The benefits of formal mentoring far outweigh the perceived limitations, all of which can be dealt with through careful planning and clearly defined objectives and expectations. If your firm is considering a mentoring program, some lawyers may object, and you will need to address their objections. The principal objections to mentoring programs are stated below, followed by responses that explain how a mentoring program can overcome the supposed limitation.

Objection: *Mentoring programs create artificial relationships that are doomed to fail.*

Response: It is true that formal mentoring relationships are artificially created, but this fact does not prevent the mentor and associate from working together to achieve their specified mentoring objectives. In a mentoring program, commitment is more important than personal chemistry. Lawyers who enter a mentoring relationship willingly, with a positive attitude, will be effective in that relationship. Ultimately, the formality of the relationship is less significant than the objectives, characteristics, and design of the program. The fact that mentors and associates are assigned to each other becomes insignificant when the program's expectations are clearly delineated and understood; when the expected mentoring efforts are viewed as reasonable and not unduly burdensome; when participants do not feel anxious or confused about their responsibilities; and when the firm provides ongoing encouragement and support.

Objection: *Mentoring programs impose conformity and a "Big Brother" atmosphere.*

Response: Program guidelines are intended to clarify expectations, prevent confusion, and offer helpful suggestions. They are not rigid requirements. To the contrary, the program should encourage mentors and associates to be creative and to approach the mentoring process in a manner most suitable and effective for their own particular styles and needs. Although the program coordinator monitors the program to ensure that the program objectives are being met, no one is "spying" on program participants, and all mentoring relationships are voluntary.

Objection: *Mentoring programs raise unrealistic expectations in associates.*

Response: To the contrary, mentoring programs manage associates' expectations better than informal mentoring. Associates do often have unrealistic expectations about what their mentors can or will do for them. A formal mentoring program controls those expectations. Unlike an informal relationship, formal mentoring delineates what the associate should realistically expect from the mentor. From the very beginning, a mentoring program uses training sessions, program guidelines, and ongoing support efforts to educate mentors and associates about the true nature and purpose of mentoring relationships.

Objection: *Mentoring programs impose unrealistic demands on mentors.*

Response: Mentors actually have an easier time in a formal program than in informal relationships because their roles are explicit and circumscribed. Programs provide training and guidelines to prepare mentors for their mentoring roles and to inform associates about the limitations of formal mentoring relationships. In most programs, mentors will find that their responsibilities are less onerous than they believe, and the benefits of mentoring are greater than they imagine.

Objection: *Mentoring is a waste because "associates are just going to leave anyway."*

Response: Many partners complain that mentoring associates merely helps the associate's next employer and that the firm's resources are better used in other pursuits. Mentoring will not guarantee that associates will stay at your firm, but failing to provide mentoring significantly increases the likelihood that they will leave. This complaint is short-sighted and runs the risk of becoming a self-fulfilling prophesy. Even if they leave, associates who have had satisfying mentoring relationships will speak well of the mentor and of the firm's mentoring endeavor. Strong mentoring relationships may also bring departing lawyers back to the firm at a later time.

Objection: *Mentoring programs take up too much non-billable time.*

Response: Mentoring need not take an inordinate amount of time. When incorporated into a lawyer's regular practice, it becomes an enjoyable and natural activity that takes little extra time and can sometimes be done in the course of billable work. Moreover, mentoring should be viewed not as a question of billable or non-billable time but as an essential long-term investment in your associates. Mentoring lets you direct and assess the professional competence of the associates who serve your clients and will one day attract their own. As David Maister has pointed out, "What you do with your billable time is revenue. What you do with your non-billable time is your future."

Objection: *Mentoring programs are not cost-effective.*

Response: Mentoring is indeed cost-effective. Mentoring can save firms hundreds of thousands of dollars a year by retaining valuable associates, and it has been shown to increase the productivity of mentors and associates, which goes right to the bottom line. (See "Raising Productivity" in Chapter 3.)

Objection: *Mentoring programs add another bureaucratic layer.*

Response: The savings from increased retention and lawyer productivity easily offset the modest administrative expense of a mentoring program. Mentoring programs do require some additional administrative support, but careful planning and efficient design can limit those costs.

CHAPTER 9

ESTABLISHING A FORMAL MENTORING PROGRAM IN YOUR FIRM

*"The real voyage of discovery consists not in
seeking new landscapes but in having new eyes."*

MARCEL PROUST

DESIGNING YOUR PROGRAM

If the conditions are right and the firm is ready, you can begin to plan your mentoring program. Having a checklist of the necessary steps and elements will ensure that you cover all the bases. *Table 7* is a checklist that contains the program elements discussed in Chapters Seven and Eight and later in this chapter. It also includes questions to consider regarding each element. A mentoring program for a large international law firm is necessarily more complicated than a program for a small office. Smaller firms may not need to follow every step (e.g., a pilot program) but should review each program element to be sure their design is complete. When using a checklist, be sure to assign tasks to specific individuals and include a timetable for completion of each task.

TABLE 7. Establishing a Mentoring Program: Checklist

A. **Leadership commitment**
- How committed are your firm leaders to a structured mentoring program?

B. **Program objectives**
- What do you want your mentoring program to achieve?
- How will a mentoring program further the firm's business strategy?
- What are your program objectives?
- Are your objectives practical, realistic, and measurable?
- Which attorneys will the program serve?
- What professional development needs will it address?

C. **Program parameters**
- How long will the mentoring relationship last?
- What types of issues and concerns are within the scope of the mentoring relationship?
- How much time should the mentor and associate spend in mentoring activities?
- What should mentoring activities include?
- How much money should mentors spend on mentoring activities?
- Who will pay for these activities?

D. **Procedure and criteria for matching mentors and associates**
- How will associates and mentors be matched?
- What criteria will be used?
- Will participants select their own mentors and/or protégés?
- Who will make the matching decision?

E. **Program management**
- Who will be your program coordinator?
- What will the program coordinator do?

F. **Training**
- What will be included in your mentoring training curriculum?
- Who will provide the training?
- When will training be given?

(continued)

G. Ongoing support and monitoring
- What kind of support will the program coordinator give to participants?
- How will the program be monitored?

H. Evaluation
- How and when will the program be evaluated?
- Who will do the evaluation?
- How will individual mentoring experiences be evaluated?
- How will success be measured?

I. Written guidelines
- Do your written guidelines cover all essential elements of the program?

J. Mentoring incentives
- How will you encourage and reward people who engage in mentoring activities?

K. Mentors
- Who are the potential mentors in your program?
- What attributes will you look for in potential mentors?
- Who can be mentors: partners? associates? retired partners? counsel? non-lawyer personnel?
- How will mentors be recruited?

L. Associates
- Which lawyers will be mentored in your program?
- Will you include all lawyers in a certain group?
- Will you limit participation to certain individuals?
- If the program will be limited, what will the selection criteria be?
- Will your program include part-time attorneys?

M. Mentor-associate relationships
- What will mentors' responsibilities be?
- What will associates' responsibilities be?
- Are mentor-associate communications confidential?
- Are there any limits on confidentiality?
- How will you deal with problems that arise in mentoring relationships?
- Will the mentor supervise the associate's work?
- If mentor and associate work together, how will that impact confidentiality?
- What will be the mentor's role in associate evaluations?

- How will the mentor be expected to handle sensitive information about the associate?
- What role, if any, will the mentor play in deciding the associate's work assignments?
- How will the mentor relate to the associate's supervising attorneys?
- How many mentors will be assigned to an associate?
- How many associates will be assigned to a mentor?

N. Pilot project

- Which individuals, groups, and offices, will be included?
- How long will the pilot project last?
- What procedure is in place to monitor and make adjustments?
- How will it be evaluated?

O. Marketing the program

- What will you use to market the program inside the firm?
- Do your materials inform and promote the program?
- Are your marketing materials designed to recruit participants for the program?
- Are your marketing materials designed to attract lawyers and clients to the firm?
- How will you launch your program?
- How will you educate your lawyers and staff about the program?
- What publicity materials will you use?

P. Integrating professional development activities

- Is your mentoring program coordinated with other professional development activities?
- Will the mentoring program coordinator coordinate any other aspects of associates' professional development?
- Will mentors play a role in coordinating any other professional development activities?

PILOT PROJECT

If you are starting a new program, it is wise to begin with a pilot project so that you can test your ideas and fine tune your design. Start with a small group. Depending on the intended scale of your program, you might choose to try a pilot project in one practice group, one small office, or a small group of individuals (e.g., third-year corporate associates). Starting small has the advantage of being easier to control because you can hand-pick initial participants and locations where you expect the most support and enthusiasm, and where the program is likeliest to succeed. It is always easier to build momentum for a program that is perceived favorably than for one that is not. As the program goes forward, you can work out the kinks and make adjustments as you go.

Watch the pilot project carefully and assess it frequently. Your program design should include evaluation tools and techniques that measure the program's effectiveness. Be sure to budget enough time to do a thorough evaluation of the pilot project. The amount of time you will need depends on the complexity and objectives of the program. The time required for a simple orientation program for new associates may be just three to six months, long enough to follow one class of new associates through the program. If, however, the mentoring program is more complex and requires more extensive observation and tracking (e.g., helping litigation associates develop trial skills), the period for the pilot project may have to be longer. If the pilot project requires a lengthy test period, you may choose to roll out the whole program, all at once or incrementally, after a reasonable period of observation and evaluation but before the pilot is completed.

LAUNCHING YOUR
MENTORING PROGRAM

You have done your background work and designed your program; you have successfully executed your pilot project; now you are ready for prime time. You are excited about the program and want to spread that enthusiasm throughout the firm. Like every other aspect of the program development process, this also requires a plan. You will want to market your program aggressively, and a well-conceived marketing plan can help you do exactly that. The plan should have three objectives: to inform, promote, and recruit. The program must be presented to the firm in a way that will inform everyone of its purpose and expectations, generate enthusiasm and momentum, build support, and inspire potential mentors and associates to participate. Even if lawyers support the notion of mentoring in the abstract, you will need to persuade them to accept the program you have designed. If assigned relationships will be narrow in scope and brief in duration, you may not have much trouble. But if the program will require a substantial amount of time and effort, you will need grass-roots support throughout the firm as well as buy-in from the top.

Building support in the firm will require you to present data that explains why the program is needed and what it is intended to accomplish. From the data you gathered in preparing for the program, you will be well prepared to articulate these reasons to the firm. Your firm-specific data will be more persuasive when supplemented by research-based reports such as the NALP Foundation's *Keeping the Keepers* study, which underscores the importance of mentoring for law firm associates.

Your internal marketing plan should include a coordinated communication strategy for publicizing the program. Use a combination of various communication techniques and media. Here are some ideas for helping you spread the word and build enthusiasm:

- Publicize the program in different forums using various written media: memos, the firm's intranet, brochures, announcements, press releases, and articles.

- Prepare a brief videotape that describes the program and its benefits. Include interviews with participants who have been in the pilot project or who have been in other mentoring relationships. Have them describe their mentoring experiences, offer helpful advice and insights, and exhort the benefits of participating in your program.

- Hold a kick-off party to inaugurate the program and invite the whole firm. At the event, identify the program coordinator, program committee, and any other key individuals. You might also use this time to answer questions about the program.

- Ask mentoring program committee members and firm leaders to promote the program. Make the job easy for them by preparing fact sheets that list the program features you want to highlight.

- Hold meetings to introduce the program in all firm offices. Invite everyone who is interested to attend. Describe the program and tell people how they can get involved.

Don't forget to publicize your program outside the firm. Mentoring is a big draw for recruits and clients. Law students and potential laterals expect firms to make professional development a priority. Clients will appreciate your firm's commitment to developing superior lawyers to serve their legal needs.

- Encourage individual lawyers to describe and promote the mentoring program in interviews with law students and prospective laterals and to clients.

- Include descriptions of the program in your recruiting materials and web site.

- Send press releases, announcements, newsletters, and brochures to law schools and clients as well as to the news media.

- Write articles for law journals and legal newspapers describing the program. Promote your program as a model for law firms.

Integrating the Mentoring Program with Other Professional Development Efforts

To be most effective, your mentoring program should be coordinated with the firm's other professional development efforts from the start. Mentoring relationships can promote, complement, and augment those efforts. If it remains separate, the mentoring program will compete for firm resources, especially attorney time and attention. Even if your mentoring program is the centerpiece of your associate development efforts, it will be more apt to succeed when it is part of a larger professional development program.

Professional development embraces everything that affects attorneys' professional growth from the time they are recruited into the firm until they retire, including:

- Training and skills development;

- Assignments;

- Work experience;

- Feedback and evaluation;

- Socialization and involvement in law firm life;

- Client relations;

- Business development;

- Administrative and management responsibilities;

- Leadership development; and

- Career planning.

The mentoring program coordinator can play a major role in coordinating and tracking associates' broader professional development. Mentors can coordinate various aspects of professional development. The extent of a mentor's involvement depends on the program's charge to the mentor and on the other professional development resources that exist in the firm. Here are some examples of how mentors can take the lead or supplement existing professional development efforts:

- Teach practices not taught in formal training programs.

- Clarify what is taught in formal training programs by answering associates' questions and explaining how lessons apply to practice.

- Ensure that associates get appropriate work experience by controlling their work assignments or coordinating efforts with the people who do.

- Give associates constructive and useful feedback concerning the work the mentors supervise directly. Participate in the evaluation and performance review process. (See Chapter Seven.)

- Encourage associates to be sociable and participate in the social life of the firm.

- Help associates learn about client development. Introduce associates to clients, supervise their work with clients, and instruct and model effective client relations. Explain how to use the firm's marketing resources to help associates locate prospective clients and market their services. Educate associates about other partners' clients and practices.

Accounting giant Deloitte & Touche is an excellent example of how mentoring as part of an integrated professional development effort can have far-reaching impact. In 1992, Deloitte realized that its turnover rate among women was 24 percent, significantly higher than the 18 percent rate for men, and extremely costly in terms of both money and lost talent. Deloitte also found that 80 percent of the women who left the firm did not leave the profession but went to other accounting firms with cultures more supportive of their needs. In response, Deloitte embarked on a comprehensive, long-term "Initiative for the Retention and Advancement of Women," with mentoring as one of its integral features. Although it was prompted by the special needs of women, Deloitte made the benefits of the Women's Initiative equally available to both women and men.

Under the Women's Initiative, employees have two mentors. Shortly after they arrive at the firm, associates are paired with a "mentor" who is available for everyday advice and a "counselor" who offers career guidance, keeps the associate on track toward promotion, and continues in this role as long as the associate works at Deloitte. These mentors use developmental benchmarks to monitor the associate's progress, track the associate's work assignments and promotions, assist with career planning and counseling, and sponsor networking activities.

One of the long-term benefits to Deloitte is a culture where men and women experience high satisfaction levels and increasingly opt to stay with the firm. Since the Women's Initiative was introduced in 1993, the number of women partners in the firm has more than doubled and their percentage has tripled. By 1998, turnover was reduced for both men and women, with an impressive decrease in women's attrition to 17 percent. Deloitte has determined that the increase in retention as a result of the Women's Initiative has saved the company $80 million.

CHAPTER 10

INFORMAL, GROUP, AND PEER MENTORING PROGRAMS

"We know what we are, but we know not what we may be."

WILLIAM SHAKESPEARE

ENHANCED INFORMAL MENTORING

Some firms or practice groups do not need a formal mentoring program because they have an environment where informal mentoring happens regularly. In these groups, partners and associates have close working relationships and associates look to the partners they work with as mentors. Associates feel that these mentoring relationships are promoting their professional development and providing stimulating and challenging work. If that is the case in your firm, there is no reason to replace these informal mentoring relationships with a formal program. Instead, build on the foundation you already have. Take steps to protect and enhance the firm's mentoring culture.

Even in the best of conditions, informal mentoring is an endangered activity. You can protect and promote informal mentoring through measures calculated to lock in its occurrence and benefits. Informal mentoring needs to be nurtured and fostered because when stress levels rise, mentoring activities decline. Lawyers are easily diverted by other pressing matters, and relationships suffer. But if mentoring becomes a natural part of everyday practice, mentoring will continue even when times are tough. When lawyers have the skills, opportunities, and encouragement to enter informal mentoring relationships, lawyers mentor each other routinely, without even thinking about it. In that way, mentoring becomes ingrained in the culture of the firm.

Regardless of how expansive informal mentoring is in your firm, some associates will not benefit. Maybe they are too shy or unaware of how to engage in mentoring relationships, or perhaps their work situation is not conducive to the formation of such relationships. Some associates will not have mentors because they are perceived (rightly or wrongly) as "losers" and partners do not want to mentor them. In a few cases, associates will have mentors but their mentoring experiences will not be satisfying. Their mentors will not meet their needs or their mentoring relationship will start off well but then falter. Your firm may have a flourishing mentoring culture but none of these associates will share in it. For this reason, it is advisable to assign certain individuals the responsibility of identifying associates who have not "connected" with mentors and helping them make those connections.

A firm where lawyers regularly have informal mentoring relationships can take some simple measures to enhance mentoring practices and keep mentoring alive. Some of these measures include:

- **Identification of potential mentors and protégés.** Keep a list of individuals who are interested in being or having a mentor and make this information available to people who need a mentoring partner.

- **Training workshops to teach lawyers mentoring skills and practices.** Encourage all lawyers to attend, including those who are not currently engaged in mentoring activities. Workshops should be held periodically throughout the year. Among other things, these workshops can show attorneys how, in the absence of a formal program, they can set mentoring goals, timetables, and a plan of action.

- **Distribution of written materials.** Written materials should supplement training, offer helpful ideas and suggestions, and remind everyone of their mentoring responsibilities. These materials might be technical articles from journals about mentoring or simple lists of tips generated in-house. Some firms circulate information in their internal newsletters or intranets about "best mentoring practices," profiles of outstanding

mentors, and descriptions of special firm-sponsored mentoring activities.

- **Conferences where mentoring issues are discussed.**
  Sponsor casual get-togethers (e.g., brown bag lunches) or
  more formal events where mentoring is the central topic. Invite
  clients to talk about mentoring in their organizations, prominent
  individuals to describe significant mentoring experiences they
  have had, or mentoring consultants to explain how to build trust.

- **Accolades and rewards for outstanding mentoring.** Excellent mentors should be recognized and publicized. Aside from
  reinforcing the importance of good mentoring, this will highlight
  practices to emulate and identify mentoring role models.

- **Designation of a firm "mentoring maven."** Designate someone to act as a resource to lawyers interested in or engaged in a
  mentoring relationship. This individual would be available to
  field questions about mentoring, help associates find a mentor,
  and help people who are having problems in a mentoring
  relationship.

Group Mentoring

Group mentoring pairs one mentor with a small group of less experienced attorneys. One senior attorney, usually a partner or other
prominent attorney, acts as a mentor to a small group of associates to
achieve specific objectives. This approach allows a single partner to
have an impact that reaches several junior lawyers at once. Group
mentoring can be a major component of the firm's mentoring program
or supplemental to it.

Group mentoring affords many benefits and a great deal of flexibility.
One positive feature is that, by working with a group, your busiest and
most sought-after mentors can maximize their exposure to associates
without overloading themselves. Group mentoring promotes relationship building among participants, fosters teamwork, and serves as an
effective forum for learning and professional growth.

The group format is also very flexible. Mentors may lead a group
singly or pair up with another mentor, and two or more mentoring
groups might also meet together from time to time. Similarly, mentors

can invite associates within the group to pair up as one-on-one peer mentors. These pairs mentor each other and may also work on special projects or presentations for the group. Within the group mentoring context, mentors have substantial autonomy over how their groups approach issues related to the mentoring program objectives. For example, your overall objective might be to help second-year associates learn how to serve clients more effectively. Within that framework, one mentor might focus on what clients expect from their lawyers by bringing in some clients to talk with the group. Another mentor might use hypothetical case studies to explore how associates should handle difficult client situations. A third mentor might decide to look at how good client relations can lead to further business.

Mentoring groups can set their own pace and meeting schedule. It is common for these groups to meet once a month for at least six months to one year, with each session lasting one to three hours. During the sessions, mentors should keep formal presentations to a minimum. Instead, they should employ more engaging teaching methods: role playing, guest presentations, case studies, audiovisual materials, and other techniques that promote dialogue. In group mentoring, the mentor's role is to facilitate group learning. This is not a natural skill, and mentors who lead mentoring groups should be given training in group dynamics, team building, and the skills needed to facilitate group involvement.

Group mentoring is formal in the sense that it is organized around an objective. That objective may be a specific desired outcome or it may be to serve or explore particular practice needs or interests. When the objective is a specific outcome (i.e., to solve a particular problem), group mentoring tends to be a more intense experience. It becomes a form of "action learning" where lawyers learn and develop professional skills while working together, under the tutelage of a mentor, to resolve a real firm problem. Participants learn how to analyze, strategize, and devise creative solutions within the law firm's context. The problems they deal with are real issues facing the firm: creating a new firm marketing campaign, developing a new approach to billing, considering whether and how the firm should expand, devising a plan for increasing associate retention, or building a new practice group.

What makes this experience unique is that the firm turns problem solving into learning through the mentoring process. Issues that would normally be addressed by a committee of partners are assigned to a select group of lawyers and a mentor. While a committee would just look for a solution, the mentor takes the group on an educational journey.

Mentors in these groups do not have the answers or solutions for the problem facing the group. Instead, mentors facilitate the learning process and bring their wisdom and experience to bear on the discussion. Most of the work — and learning — happens in the group. Although the mentor leads the group, group members are expected to take an active part, and, consequently, they learn from each other as well. Mentors offer direction and stimulation; they question, provoke, and challenge. Some mentors use historical experiences to raise or illustrate points, present hypotheticals to solicit various viewpoints or spark a debate, or assign pertinent readings about the issue. During these sessions, participants probe, question, learn, and grow. In this learning process, the mentor and the group reach a deeper understanding of the firm's needs, systems, and dynamics.

The length of sessions and the duration of the group mentoring process depends on the issues the group deals with and on how long it takes them to find solutions. The mentor and the group decide together how much time they will spend and how that time will be used. Because the issues are real for the firm, the group frequently operates under imposed deadlines.

This type of mentoring lends itself well to programs for senior associates and junior partners. The nature of the work done by the group and the involvement of the firm's prominent attorneys as mentors make this an excellent forum for leadership development. Participants learn to critically analyze their own behaviors and assumptions, assess how they define and solve problems, and examine why things happen as they do. They reflect on their own experiences, gain new insights into the policy-making process, and learn the dynamics of teamwork. The group's efforts are important to the business of the firm as well as to the development of its lawyers. These group mentoring programs bring talented lawyers into the firm's leadership circle and prepare them to take over the leadership reins.

Most group mentoring experiences are not as focused or intense as outcome-based group mentoring. In its more common form, rather than solving a particular law firm problem, group mentoring deals with issues of legal practice and professional development. Mentoring groups may decide their own objectives or objectives can be set by the firm. Objectives typically focus on work and career issues, but those issues can cover a wide range of topics (e.g., career advancement strategies, practice dilemmas, substantive legal issues, work-life balance).

Group mentoring is an especially effective way to give minority associates access to minority mentors. Mentoring groups comprised only of minority attorneys can create important development and support networks, as well as direct access to minority partners and role models in the firm. However, keep in mind that race-based mentoring groups within a firm have risks as well as benefits.[1] The benefits of such groups are numerous and include:

- A safe environment to discuss career concerns;

- Opportunities to freely discuss how others perceive minority attorneys in light of stereotypes and expectations;

- Opportunities to explore strategies for dealing with work and interpersonal problems;

- Confirmation that differences can be assets;

- Formation of business and professional networks;

- Confidence building;

- Informing the firm about issues facing members of the group;

- Bringing the contributions of group members to the attention of the firm;

- Spotlighting group members who can be mentors and role models for other minority attorneys; and

- Promoting business from minority clients.

In contrast, the risks of having an all-minority mentoring group are that:

- An exclusionary group may undermine the firm's goal of diversity.

- Others may be suspicious of the group.

- Others may perceive that the group needs special remedial help, reinforcing the stereotype that minority attorneys are less competent.

---

[1] Ida Abbott, "Mentoring Plays a Key Role in Retaining Attorneys of Color," *Law Governance Review*, Spring 1998.

The firm cannot presume that any of its minority attorneys want to be in an all-minority mentoring group. The firm needs to elicit minority attorneys' opinions and desires on this question in a sensitive way. If some minority attorneys want an all-minority mentoring group, the firm should try to accommodate them. If your firm has such a mentoring group, it is critical to maintain an environment where attorneys feel comfortable and supported when they participate. The most important point, however, is that all-minority mentoring groups should supplement, not supplant, other mentoring activities in the firm. This form of mentoring should not be seen as a substitute for minority associates' access to individual mentors of any race or ethnicity in the firm.

PEER MENTORING

Peer mentoring is a non-hierarchical form of mentoring in which colleagues mentor and learn from each other. Peer mentors can perform any or all of the functions of traditional mentors. What distinguishes peer mentoring from traditional mentoring is that, for purposes of the mentoring relationship, participants are on an equal footing, even when one has more seniority in rank or experience. Peer mentoring emphasizes a learning dialogue between a pair of colleagues or within a small and collegial group. This form of mentoring is commonplace in law firms and occurs on a daily basis when lawyers seek career help and advice from each other. Peer mentoring is especially appealing for lawyers in solo or small practices because peer mentors need not be in the same firm. They may be former law school classmates, colleagues in another firm, or any lawyers with whom you have a good relationship. Because any two or more people can freely form a group, peer mentoring opportunities are unlimited.

In one-on-one relationships, peer mentors act as counselors and sounding boards for each other. They do this on a regular basis with or without formal meetings. For example, associates get together to discuss a problem partner; two women attorneys compare notes about work and child care schedules; two senior partners discuss how to keep up productivity as their energy for law practice wanes. In all of these settings, lawyers are willing to listen, commiserate, and offer support and advice to their colleagues. Although one of the two may take the primary lead as the mentor, it is not unusual for each to act as a mentor to the other.

The other way that peer mentoring occurs is in small groups. Peers identify business or professional competencies they would like to develop, issues they would like to explore, or problems they would like to solve. They meet regularly to exchange ideas and information, learn from one another, offer encouragement, and develop strategies to achieve professional goals. They set their own agenda, which may include presentations by outside speakers or "homework" assignments (e.g., reading articles, finding contacts, or locating examples of what others in the field have done). They may keep their meetings informal or structure them, with members rotating responsibility for leading the discussion. The key to a peer mentoring group is that each member of the group has something to offer as well as to learn, so each person is a mentor and a protégé.

Whether it is one-on-one or in a small group, peer mentoring benefits lawyers at all experience levels. In fact, while conventional (i.e., more senior) mentors are deemed to be most important in early career development when advancement is at stake, peer mentors are important at all career stages. Peer mentoring is particularly valuable for lawyers who want to address shared professional or developmental issues but who do not have suitable mentors in their firm or organization. For lawyers with special career needs or who face special issues (e.g., women, minority, gay, and lesbian attorneys), peer groups also create important support networks. Because these lawyers may lack access to many of the informal support networks and communication channels in the firm, peer mentoring enables them to discuss career challenges and issues of mutual concern with supportive and sympathetic colleagues.

Peer mentoring groups can be the basis of a mentoring program, or they can supplement one-on-one mentoring programs. Peer-to-peer groups are also available to lawyers through bar associations and other professional and business organizations in many communities. An excellent example is the "mentoring circles" program started by the New York Women's Bar Association in 1994. Intended to promote the career and personal development of women attorneys, each mentoring circle consisted of six to eight women from a wide variety of backgrounds spanning private, corporate, non-profit, judicial, and government practice. Each woman brought different talents, perspectives, and insights to her group, and the women's differences enriched the mentoring experience.

The life cycle of peer mentoring groups is open ended, and it is not uncommon for peer mentoring groups to continue for many years. When members like each other and continue to derive professional benefits from their group, their interest and motivation remain high. Of the five New York Women's Bar Association mentoring circles formed in 1994, three were still meeting in 1999.

CHAPTER 11

SPECIAL MENTORING PROGRAM ISSUES AND CONSIDERATIONS

"The ability to learn may be the only
sustainable competitive advantage."

ARIE DE GEUS

CORPORATE LEGAL DEPARTMENTS

Corporate legal departments are well suited for mentoring. Operating within the formal hierarchy of the company, an in-house lawyer's career path typically ascends into a management position. Attaining management status in a legal department requires that a lawyer possess effective management skills, many of which are the same skills used by mentors (e.g., coaching, feedback, supervision). In many corporations, management training is provided for lawyers who become managers.

Within the legal department, lawyer-managers have a more formal supervisory relationship with the other lawyers in their group, which facilitates mentoring. These managers monitor the work product, performance, and professional development of the lawyers who report to them, and are responsible for seeing that those lawyers have good technical skills, understand the company's business, and work effectively with the company's business people. Many managers are evaluated and promoted on the basis of how well they manage and develop the lawyers they supervise, so they have a personal stake in their professional development. As one Associate General Counsel for an international bank explained, "There is no bell curve in my group. I want every lawyer here to be outstanding."

Yet little informal mentoring occurs within corporate law departments. Legal departments face issues regarding professional training, development, and advancement similar to those of private law firms. They also have similar problems that inhibit mentoring — e.g., poor communication and lack of interaction among lawyers. However, many corporate counsel find informal mentors outside the legal department on the business side of company, and these mentors are just as important as legal mentors. Corporate lawyers have to understand the company's business, and they need access to the company's business expertise and resources. Mentors from the business side help lawyers learn about corporate areas and functions with which they may not be familiar. These cross-functional mentoring relationships foster trust, confidence, and collaboration between the company and its lawyers. Having a network of mentors throughout the organization therefore increases the lawyer's effectiveness.

Mentoring relationships also expand lawyers' career opportunities. Because there are usually very few management positions at the top of the legal department for counsel who aspire to become managers, many corporate lawyers move to the business side of the company and advance in other corporate departments. A network of mentors provides a lawyer with inside information about job opportunities and makes it easier for the lawyer to move into other departments. The company benefits by retaining capable lawyers and promoting and transforming them into business managers and executives.

Many corporations have formal mentoring programs designed to further the professional development and advancement of employees, which may include lawyers. Common objectives of these programs are to develop and retain key employees, educate employees about business aspects of the company, broaden the internal networks and bonds among employees, promote work force diversity, plan for leadership succession, increase collaboration among departments, and improve employee morale and productivity. But legal departments frequently fail to be included in, or to avail themselves of, those programs.

Many corporate mentoring programs deliberately pair employees with mentors from other departments. They encourage employees to develop a network of colleagues from other parts of the company. This benefits the company by expanding communication channels and disseminating information more widely, and benefits participants by exposing them to growth opportunities in other parts of the company. Participants follow each other's careers and serve as important contacts for each other as they advance up the corporate ladder.

This prospect is even greater when group mentoring is part of the program. Many corporate programs commonly pair a select group of high-potential employees as protégés with mentors who are company executives. These programs may also hold peer mentoring sessions for groups of protégés. Members of the protégé group share with each other what they learn in their mentoring relationships with executives, and each executive mentor in the program meets once or twice with the entire protégé group. In many cases, the relationships formed within the protégé group have a greater impact on protégés' careers than their relationships with individual mentors.

Lawyers may or may not qualify for the mentoring programs sponsored by their companies, depending on the scope and intent of particular programs. Lawyers in companies which have mentoring programs should check with the Human Resources Department to find out if formal mentoring is available to them, or to suggest that the corporation begin a mentoring program in which lawyers can participate. Lawyers who wish to establish a mentoring program within the legal department can use the principles and steps discussed in Chapters Six through Ten.

Solo Practitioners, Small Firms, and Small Legal Departments

Mentoring is important for lawyers who work alone, in small firms, and in small corporate or government legal departments. For these lawyers, creating a network of mentors is an especially worthwhile strategy. If you do not have a ready source of mentors in your workplace, Chapter Five, which explains how to find mentors, should be helpful. You can look for individual mentors or start your own peer mentoring group as described in Chapter Ten, by inviting some colleagues who share your professional interests or needs to participate. In addition, there are many established mentoring programs which may be available to you.

■ Many national, state, local, and specialty bar associations have mentoring programs. Usually, other members of the organization volunteer to act as mentors for new lawyers or for lawyers in need of mentoring assistance. The State Bar of Texas, for example, provides experienced volunteer mentors for inexperienced lawyers and solo practitioners.

■ Law school alumni associations frequently have mentoring programs or provide mentoring opportunities.

■ The Small Business Administration, chambers of commerce, and other business and professional groups sponsor individualized, group, and peer mentoring programs, as well as networking opportunities where lawyers can find potential mentors.

■ Private organizations such as Menttium and WOMEN, Unlimited, sponsor mentoring opportunities for women.

■ Chat rooms on web sites for lawyers are good places to find answers to practice questions and discussion groups for lawyers who share common interests. Electronic mentoring can be useful for limited purposes as a later section of this chapter describes.

Favoritism, Jealousy, and Other "Perception" Issues

Mentoring may arouse strong emotional reactions in people who are not involved in the mentoring program. It is part of human nature that people who observe a close working relationship between two other people may feel excluded, envious, resentful, or jealous. This emotional backlash can take many forms. When a mentor creates new opportunities for an assigned associate that are not available to others, the others may be resentful. Associates may believe that the mentored associate is receiving favored treatment. Partners not in the program may believe that mentors have unfair access to associates for work assignments.

Your best approach is to try to prevent these negative perceptions from arising in the first place. To do this, be clear in explaining the purpose, criteria for participation, and parameters of the mentoring program and make your program as open as possible to as many lawyers as possible.

When people in the firm express negative feelings toward the program or participants, it is important to address their concerns. Most of the time, this should be done privately, but if the concerns involve the overall operation of the program, an open forum may be a better place to air the issues.

Electronic Mentoring

The increasing expansion, consolidation, and globalization of law firms means that lawyers in the same firm may be located all over the world. In some mentoring programs, the best mentoring matches may involve lawyers who are in offices that are hundreds or thousands of miles apart. In those circumstances, electronic mentoring ("e-mentoring") can be an expedient way for them to communicate. E-mentoring uses technology to form, maintain, and facilitate mentoring relationships. E-mentoring is becoming more and more common in educational institutions and corporations and is being used increasingly to pair professionals with on-line mentors in their fields.

Technology can facilitate and support your mentoring program in many ways. On-line training sessions can be used for some aspects of training for program participants. A web-accessed chat room can enable participants to communicate and share questions, experience, and advice. An intranet or web site can be a resource for posting mentoring tips, tools, procedures, and resources. In practices where lawyers are always on the road, mentors and associates can stay in touch through email and video-conferencing.

The uses for technology in mentoring are far-reaching, but technology alone makes for an incomplete and not fully satisfying mentoring experience. As with most personal relationships, some face-to-face contact between mentor and associate adds texture, depth, and feeling that are missing in electronic communications. While some mentoring functions, such as sharing information about work and career opportunities or giving associates "pep talks" and encouragement, adapt well to e-mentoring, other functions, such as helping an associate with a performance problem, a difficult client, or other emotional and anxiety-provoking situations, are more effective when handled in person. Unless it is impossible because of the nature of your practice or the geographical distribution of your lawyers, mentors and their assigned associates should meet in person at least from time to time.

TERMINOLOGY: WHAT TO CALL YOUR MENTORS AND YOUR PROGRAM

Give careful thought to what you will call the mentors in your program. Although this may sound trivial, it will make a difference in how receptive people will be to the program. Of course what matters most is the function, not the title, of the mentor, but the nomenclature you use should reflect and be compatible with the culture of your firm. Some lawyers will recoil when you mention a mentoring program, either because of their own bad mentoring experiences or because they feel the term has been so overused that it has become meaningless. This may be a particularly sensitive point if the firm has previously tried mentoring programs without success. The same lawyers may respond more favorably if they are called "coaches," "counselors," "advisors," or "sponsors" instead of mentors.

The objectives you have established for your program may suggest the terminology to use. If the mentor's role will be to help the associate achieve developmental goals or improve performance, "coach" may be a good alternative to "mentor." If the mentor's focus will be on career guidance and advice, the term "advisor" or "counselor" may be more apt. If the mentor will be preparing senior associates for partnership, then "sponsor" might be a good choice.

You might also want to give your program a descriptive title. A name for the program that reflects its purpose may provide a convenient shorthand way to talk about it. At King & Spalding, the mentoring program is designed to "link" lawyers to each other and to the firm. Mid-level associates are assigned as mentors to new and lateral associates, and the pair are also assigned to a partner who acts as a mentor. To reflect this emphasis on forging multiple relationships, the firm calls its mentoring program the "Link Program."

USE OF OUTSIDE CONSULTANTS

Most mentoring programs can be developed and implemented entirely by the firm. However, outside consultants can be very helpful resources. With their expertise in mentoring, human resources, and organizational development, they can help you at every stage in planning and implementing your mentoring program. Some of the ways that outside consultants can be helpful include the following:

- **Evaluating the culture of your firm for receptivity to a formal mentoring program.** Third parties can help you perform a "cultural audit" to determine the firm's readiness for a mentoring program. If the firm needs to make cultural changes, change management consultants have the expertise and neutrality to help you design and direct the effort.

- **Training in mentoring skills.** Lawyers in your firm may be excellent mentors, but that does not mean they are able to teach others how to engage in mentoring relationships. The firm may not have the expertise or time to develop its own training programs for mentors and associates. Outside consultants can provide this training.

- **Supplementing career planning advice given by mentors.** Lawyers, even the most successful partners, are not necessarily the best career counselors. Outside professionals can offer expert guidance about career development strategies.

- **Publishing newsletters or bulletins about your mentoring program.** Most firms rely on an administrator, marketing director, lawyer, or program coordinator to handle newsletters, updates and reminders, but outside vendors can ease the time burden on office personnel.

- **Identifying causes of high associate attrition.** Lawyers in a firm may be too close to the issues to see the real reasons why associates are leaving. Consultants can be more objective and can obtain vital information that lawyers in the firm may not be able to elicit. Lawyers currently in the firm may be more candid and forthcoming with an independent consultant than with a law firm partner or administrator. Consultants can conduct exit interviews when lawyers leave the firm and obtain feedback from lawyers who recently left the firm and whom the firm regrets losing. They can ask former lawyers why they left, whether they still feel their reasons for leaving were valid, what their experience has been in their new endeavors, and what they can suggest to the firm to prevent other lawyers from leaving. (This post-exit interview procedure has the added benefit of keeping the door open for any of those lawyers who might be interested in returning to the firm.) All of this information is necessary to produce a clear and accurate picture of the reasons for attrition.

- **Monitoring and evaluating your mentoring program.** This is another area where an independent consultant can elicit sensitive information that lawyers might not feel comfortable divulging to someone inside the firm. Especially when the consultant can promise confidentiality, the firm will recover more reliable data about how mentoring relationships are working.

Not every firm will want or need to involve an outside consultant. You may have sufficient resources within the firm to do all the tasks required for a mentoring program, and hiring an outside person adds to your expense. But if your firm's personnel or time resources are insufficient, or if you are concerned about candor and reliability when gathering data relevant to the program, an outside consultant can be a big help.

REFERENCES

"A Graduate's Legacy: On the Importance of Mentoring," *Hastings Community*, Summer, 1999.

Abbott, Ida, "Mentoring Plays a Key Role in Retaining Attorneys of Color," *Law Governance Review*, Spring, 1998.

Bass, Patricia W., "Law School Enrollment and Employment for Women and People of Color," *Diversity & The Bar*, Minority Corporate Counsel Association, August, 1999.

Butler, Timothy, and Waldroop, James, "Job Sculpting: The Art of Retaining Your Best People," *Harvard Business Review*, September-October, 1999.

Catalyst, "Women of Color in Corporate Management: Opportunities and Barriers," New York, 1999.

Catalyst, *Advancing Women in Business: The Catalyst Guide*, Jossey-Bass Publishers, San Francisco, 1998.

Catalyst, "Women in Corporate Leadership: Progress and Prospects," New York, 1996.

Catalyst, "Mentoring: A Guide to Corporate Programs and Practices," New York, 1993.

Chao, Georgia T., and Gardner, Philip D., "Formal and Informal Mentorships: A Comparison on [sic] Mentoring Functions and Contrast with Nonmentored Counterparts," *Personnel Psychology*, 45, 1992.

Daloz, Laurent A., *Mentor: Guiding the Journey of Adult Mentors*, Jossey-Bass Publishers, San Francisco, 1999.

"Diversity in the Executive Suite: Creating Successful Career Paths and Strategies," Korn/Ferry International, in conjunction with Columbia Business School, 1998.

Dreher, George F., and Ash, Ronald A., "A Comparative Study of Mentoring Among Men and Women in Managerial, Professional, and Technical Positions," *Journal of Applied Psychology*, Vol. 75, No. 5, 1990.

"1999 Emerging Work Force Study," Interim Services Inc. and Louis Harris Associates, 1999.

Facing the Grail: Confronting the Cost of Work-Family Imbalance, Boston Bar Association, 1999.

Hallowell, Edward, "The Human Moment at Work," *Harvard Business Review*, January-February, 1999.

Herzberg, Frederick, "One More Time: How Do You Motivate Employees?", *Harvard Business Review*, September-October, 1987.

Hill, Linda A., *Becoming a Manager: Mastery of a New Identity*, Penguin Books, New York, 1993.

Kanter, Rosabeth Moss, *Men and Women of the Corporation*, Basic Books, New York, 1977.

Keeping the Keepers: Strategies for Associate Retention in Times of Attrition, National Association for Law Placement (NALP) Foundation for Research and Education, Washington, D.C., 1998.

Kelley, Robert E., *How to Be a Star at Work*, Random House, New York, 1998.

Kram, Kathy, *Mentoring at Work,* Scott Foresman & Co., Glenview, Illinois, 1985.

Lindsey, Jonathan, and Eichbaum, June, "Lateral Partner Satisfaction," Major, Hagen & Africa, 1997.

Loeb, Marshall, "The New Mentoring," *Fortune Magazine*, November 27, 1995, p. 213.

McCall, Morgan W., Jr., Lombardo, Michael M., and Morrison, Ann M., *The Lessons of Experience*, The Free Press, New York, 1988.

Mullen, Ellen J., "Vocational and Psychosocial Mentoring Functions: Identifying Mentors Who Serve Both," *Human Resources Development Quarterly*, Vol. 9, No. 4, Winter, 1998.

Murray, Margo, *Beyond the Myths and Magic of Mentoring*, Jossey-Bass Publishers, San Francisco, 1991.

Ohlott, P. J., and Hughes-James, M. W., "Single-Gender and Single-Race Leadership Development Programs," *Leadership in Action*, Center for Creative Leadership and Jossey-Bass Publishers, Vol. 17, No. 4, 1997.

Perceptions of Partnership: The Allure & Accessibility of the Brass Ring, National Association for Law Placement (NALP) Foundation for Research and Education, Washington, D.C., 1999.

Phillips-Jones, Linda, "The Mentor's Guide," 1998.

Pigott, Jane, and Nowlan, Stephen E., "Success Strategies from Women at the Top," *Diversity & The Bar*, Minority Corporate Counsel Association, August, 1999.

Ragins, Belle Rose, "Diversified Mentoring Relationships in Organizations: A Power Perspective," *Academy of Management Review*, Vol. 22, No. 2, 1997.

Ruderman, M. N., Ohlott, P. J., Panzer, K., and King, S. N., "How Managers View Success: Perspectives of High Achieving Women," *Leadership in Action*, Center for Creative Leadership and Jossey-Bass Publishers, Vol. 18, No. 6, 1999.

Scandura, Terri A., "Mentorship and Career Mobility: An Empirical Investigation," *Journal of Organizational Behavior*, Vol. 13, 1992.

Scandura, Terri A., "Mentoring: The Key to Career Success," American Woman's Society of Certified Public Accountants, 1992.

Schiltz, Patrick J., "On Being Happy, Healthy, and Ethical," *Vanderbilt Law Review*, May, 1999.

Stephenson, Karen, "Diversity: A Managerial Paradox," *Clinical Sociology Review*, 1994.

Thomas, David A., and Gabarro, John J., *Breaking Through: The Making Of Minority Executives in Corporate America*, Harvard Business School Press, 1999.

Wilkins, David, "Why Are There So Few Black Lawyers?", *California Law Review*, Vol. 84, 1996.

ABOUT THE NEW YORK WOMEN'S BAR ASSOCIATION FOUNDATION, INC.

The New York Women's Bar Association Foundation, Inc., founded in 1995, is a Section 501(c) (3) tax-exempt charitable organization whose mission is to: (1) eliminate gender bias and other forms of discrimination from the legal system and legal profession, (2) promote the social and economic equality, safety and well being of women and children, and (3) address the unmet legal needs of women and children. In addition to its mentoring project, the Foundation has established a summer fellowship program sponsoring law student internships at public interest organizations (beginning in Summer 2000 with The Lawyers Committee for Human Rights) and co-sponsored with the NY Women's Bar Association, Take Your Daughter to Work Day events in the New York State Courts.

ABOUT NALP

Founded in 1971, the National Association for Law Placement, Inc., (NALP) is a non-profit alliance of ABA-accredited law schools and the nation's legal employers. Long known for its commitment to providing direct support for all stakeholders in the legal recruitment and hiring process, the National Association for Law Placement established the NALP Foundation for Research and Education in 1996. Recognized as a 501(c)(3) organization, the NALP Foundation is dedicated to advancing knowledge of law careers and the law as a profession through research and education. The NALP Foundation released its first major research report, *Keeping the Keepers: Strategies for Associate Retention in Times of Attrition*, in 1998, and its second major report, *Perceptions of Partnership: The Allure and Accessibility of the Brass Ring*, in 1999.